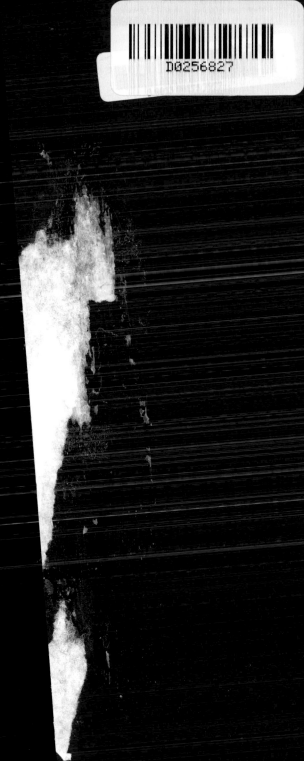

BANG! YOU'RE DEAD

Tom and Martin (2001)
Photograph: Jenny Matthews

BANG! YOU'RE DEAD

Tom Pey

JOHN WILEY & SONS, LTD
Chichester · New York · Weinheim · Brisbane · Singapore · Toronto

Published in 2001 by   John Wiley & Sons Ltd,
Baffins Lane, Chichester,
West Sussex PO19 1UD, England

National   01243 779777
International   (+44) 1243 779777
e-mail (for orders and customer service enquiries):
cs-books@wiley.co.uk
Visit our Home Page on http://www.wiley.co.uk

Photographs by Bruno Ehrs.

Other Wiley Editorial Offices

John Wiley & Sons, Inc., 605 Third Avenue,
New York, NY 10158-0012, USA

Wiley-VCH Verlag GmbH, Pappelallee 3,
D-69469 Weinheim, Germany

John Wiley & Sons Australia, Ltd, 33 Park Road, Milton,
Queensland 4064, Australia

John Wiley & Sons (Asia) Pte Ltd, 2 Clementi Loop #02-01,
Jin Xing Distripark, Singapore 129809

John Wiley & Sons (Canada) Ltd, 22 Worcester Road,
Rexdale, Ontario M9W 1L1, Canada

British Library Cataloguing in Publication Data

Library of Congress Cataloging-in-Publication Data
Pey, Tom.
   Bang! you're dead/Tom Pey.
     p. cm.
   ISBN 0-471-49692-8
   1. Pey, Tom. 2. Blind—Great Britain—Biography.
HV1947.P49 A3 2001
362.4′1′092—dc21
[B]   2001026644

A catalogue record for this book is available from the British Library

ISBN 0-471-49692-8

Typeset in 10.5/15pt Melior by Footnote Graphics, Warminster, Wiltshire
Printed and bound in Great Britain by Biddles Ltd, Guildford and King's Lynn.

This book is printed on acid-free paper responsibly manufactured from sustainable
forestry, in which at least two trees are planted for each one used for paper production.

Top Mimi and I relaxing at home (Christmas 1998)
Middle My boys: Adrian, Stephen and me (1999)
Bottom My family: Sam, Dad, me, Tony, Ma, Brendan, Dor and Breda (1994)

Dad and me, just before a concert in Birr (1965)

To my sons, Stephen and Adrian
with my eternal gratitude for their love
and for making me so proud of them

To Mimi
for her love, understanding and support
of this petulant child

**To Wendy Craddock, Andy Taylor
and Brian Cooney**
for their compassion towards a man
who was all but broken

With gratitude

My most heartfelt thanks goes to those wonderful organizations the Guide Dogs for the Blind Association and Action for Blind People, who have chosen to recognize my ability and have given me an opportunity to help

I will never forget the patience of Pam Stevens, who endured the writing and rewriting of this book and who never complained. She is a wonderful typist, secretary and friend

This book is an account of my life to date. However, a lot of the people who have touched me over the years have not sought public attention. For this reason their names have been changed to protect their privacy. Although I am an employee of the Guide Dogs for the Blind Association, any views expressed in this book are privately held and should not be attributed in any way to the Association, its Management or its Trustees.

Prologue

Baltimore USA
October 1991

It was a day like any other day, bright sunshine yet not too hot. It was a trip like countless others I had made. I caught a plane from Heathrow to Baltimore and took a taxi from the airport to my hotel. But this was no ordinary trip. Here in this city of Baltimore, revered in many Irish emigrant songs, I was to learn something that was to devastate my life and render it unrecognisable from anything I had ever thought of as acceptable.

'Are you visiting the hospital, sir?' the receptionist asked. His smile was a little too wide.

'Why?' I asked sharply.

'We have a special discount for people visiting the hospital,' he explained. He was used to his guests denying their need to visit one of the best hospitals in the world.

'Yes,' I told him quietly.

He ticked a box and handed me my key. 'Have a nice stay, sir.' He guessed this was impossible in my case.

The entrance to Johns Hopkins was monastic and reassuring. The inside was like that of the Temple of Jerusalem before Jesus cleared it of traders. Intent-looking people filed hymenopterously to programmed and well-signposted destinations, content to be categorized by their ailments, hoping for a miracle. I became one with them. My stomach churned. I wanted to go home and forget everything.

'Can I help you, sir?' She was petite, blonde and very attractive. I loved the way she said 'sir'.

'I'm looking for Doctor Fine's office,' I replied.

'Professor Fine's rooms are on the second floor. Would you like me to take you there?' I followed her to the lift.

'You work here?' I asked.

'Just started. My job is to help people who seem lost.'

'You mean, like disabled people?'

She heard the acid in my voice. 'Sometimes. But lots of people get lost here. It's a big place.'

I wanted to snap at her. But I smiled instead. 'Sorry. I'm just a little tense.'

'That's okay.' She sounded reassuring. 'Anyway, here's Professor Fine's rooms. His secretary will take care of you. Have a nice day, sir.'

Fine's secretary was tall, dark-haired and wore an expensive suit. Her gold-rimmed spectacles rested on her matched silk blouse, suspended from a gold chain, almost certainly Tiffany. She complemented the pale blue and rosewood decor. It was like the anteroom to a banker's office. Calm and designed to build confidence.

'Mister Pey?' She came from behind her imitation Louis XIV desk and shook my hand. 'Professor Fine is expecting you.' She directed me through a nearby door and into a surprisingly small and untidy office. 'Mister Pey for you,' she announced.

Fine was tall, athletic and good-looking. He grabbed my hand and squeezed with the ferocity of a bear. 'All right if I call you Tom?'

'Sure.'

'Right, Tom. There are no miracles in medicine. Not yet anyway.'

I wanted to punch his lights out. For the past twenty-four hours I had prayed for a miracle. Was this God's way of telling me he'd decided against it. He smiled. I didn't.

'I've read the notes from Ralph Rosenthal. Pity he didn't get to you sooner.'

'Look, you son of a bitch, I've come a long way. Just tell me something I don't know!'

'All I meant was I think you may have missed the boat.' He chuckled. 'What I propose to do is to take a look at the back of your eyes. If the damage is not too close to the centre, I'll operate. Okay?'

'That's what Professor Rosenthal said,' I replied testily.

'Ralph sent you here because we have the best equipment in the world. If anything can be done, we'll do it.'

'I know, Professor. It's just …'

'I know. But there are worse things in life than losing your sight.'

I laughed. 'Have you tried it?' I sneered.

Fine remained silent for just long enough to make me feel that my anger was somehow unreasonable or unmanly. I wanted to scream my rage at him but I chose silence instead. I still clung to the faint hope that a miracle might occur. 'Sorry Professor. I just remembered somebody.'

Aunt Lil was a tall, skinny woman with a big nose and a laugh that warmed your heart and made you want to giggle. She always wore a black dress covered by a navy apron dotted with off-red flowers. Her thick, grey nylons gathered around her spindly ankles and lay like Michelin curves on her unpolished, once-black lace-ups. But what did she care what she looked like? She was blind.

3

'Blind on the outside,' she would tell my sister and me.

'What d'ya mean, Aunt Lil?' my sister would ask. Assumpta, Sam, was eleven and three years older than me. Aunt Lil, she told me, was a hundred from the day she was born.

'Ya mean she was born with those wrinkles?' I asked.

She nodded. 'So were you,' she laughed. I gave her a dead arm. 'I'll tell mammy,' she cried, and hit me behind the left ear.

'Ye little divils,' Aunt Lil swore. 'I'll be dug out of ye.' Then she started to laugh.

We joined in.

'Tell us about Padraig Pearse,' my sister said. She poked me in the arm and sniggered behind her hand.

We loved the story of Padraig Pearse. The way he spent the last night in his cell writing to his mammy before the British shot him on account of him leading a revolution for Irish freedom. Aunt Lil told the story as if she knew him personally.

'A lovely man,' she said, her voice far away. 'But a bit of an eejit if ya ask me.'

'Why's that, Aunt Lil?' says I.

'Sure he must have been blinder than me to think he could get away with a stunt like that.'

'Why? Wasn't he a teacher?'

'Teachers can be blind too, young Tom. But Pearse wasn't my sort of blind. He was just an eejit.'

Silence.

'Naw. He was no eejit. He died for what he believed in.'

'There are none so blind,' she pronounced wisely, 'as those who will not see.'

Professor Fine handed me over to his team of white-coated students, who instantly found a vein in my arm and began filling me with a yellow dye. 'This will allow us to find any leaks,' one of them explained. I knew this from previous treatments. The dye made my pee turn yellow for hours afterwards.

'Is it true they use this stuff to spot leaks in drains?' I asked. A Chinese attendant laughed but didn't offer a denial.

Two hours later, after many lenses were stuck against my eye, lights shone and flashes flashed, I was guided to a waiting room. The dye had made my temperature rise and I was feeling a little nauseous.

The room was large, square and painted a fashionable grey. The afternoon sun shone through full-length, heavy net curtains. I tried to see the outside world but it was dissolved in a silky mesh. I wondered if this was what blindness was like.

I sat on one of the three overstuffed white couches that were arranged in the centre of the room like a first-class departure lounge. There was a floor-to-ceiling smoked-glass mirror directly opposite. I decided the dye had not turned my skin yellow.

I looked nervous. But only I would have known. I had practised how not to show what I was thinking. In my line of work the slightest blink could cost you money. It also helped me not to think ahead. All I had to do was wait another hour. Then I would know. Dear God, I know I don't have the right. But ... Christ! Blind? No. He'll never let it happen. I could hear the priests back in Ireland preaching their guilt-ridden piety. 'Ask the Blessed Virgin to intervene,' they would have advised. But where were She and God?

The hour passed like a week. I was thirsty and my head hurt, and I was sorry I had come to this place. My palms were moist and the knot in my stomach moved towards my neck. What in God's name is keeping you? I thought. You know I don't want to hear what you have to say—even if it's good news!

No that's not true. Please God, let it be all right. I promise I'll go to Mass on Sundays and all that. Just don't let this happen to me.

I made the sign of the Cross as if I was shaking my hands on a deal. I instantly relaxed—but only for a few seconds. Then the panic began again.

'Oh shut up,' I said angrily to the reflection in the mirror. 'Face this like a man.'

Silence.

'Man my arse,' I cried, 'I have a career, a wife and family. What will happen to them?' I searched for water and found none. My mouth felt like sandpaper and I could not hide from my panic anymore. 'Bastards,' I shouted at the whole world but at no one in particular. 'I'll show ya.'

The door opened and a doctor entered. She was young, wore a white coat but did not have a stethoscope around her neck. She had the detached look of a real professional. The slim brown file under her arm contained the rest of my life. 'We have the results of your tests,' she said. I nodded. My palms were cold. She started talking in medical speak.

'Sorry,' I interrupted, 'can we talk English.'

She smiled. 'Of course. The bottom line?'

'Please.'

'There's nothing we can do. I'm sorry.'

'Will I go blind?'

'Yes.'

'When?'

'The process has already started. You will require assistance reading in weeks. Then …'

'Then what?'

'Mister Pey, I recommend that you ...'

'What? Just stop seeing. Learn Braille? What do you recommend, Doctor?'

She touched my arm. 'You are a resilient man. Just learn how to accept.'

A million thoughts went through my mind, all at once. I now call this God's time; a time when all the imponderables flash through your mind but you don't have sufficient space in your head to contemplate the consequences of any of them, but you seem to have visited the horrors, however briefly.

'Do you have any questions?' she asked.

I pushed my hair back with both hands and desperately searched for something important to ask. My hair felt dry and my scalp felt as if it was somewhere other than on my head.

'Will I be able to watch television?'

The plane journey back to Heathrow was the loneliest of my life. I cursed God if He ever existed and I cursed myself for being so feeble as to ask the doctor such an unimportant question. But by the time we had touched down I had arrived at a number of decisions. Firstly I was going to see Professor Rosenthal in Leicester. I needed to really understand what was causing this. Secondly, and most importantly, I was going to conceal my plight from the outside world for as long as it took for me to make enough money to take care of my family. The world of finance was, after all, no place to peddle damaged goods! Thirdly, I was going to get pissed out of my head.

Chapter One

Birr, County Offaly

June 22, 1953

A westerly wind blew low across the Bog of Allen, disturbing the sleeping heathers, causing the otters to nestle closer to their watery beds. It travelled along the Athlone road, around the spire of Tom Mitchell's church and buffeted the windows of my parents' room.

The fire in the grate burned a bright yellow flecked with indigo, and a straying wisp of smoke scented the bedroom with the familiar aroma of burning peat.

My mother lay exhausted in her bed, her dark, permed hair knotted with the sweat of her labour. She felt both relieved and proud that she had given birth to her second child in the sixth year of marriage. 'A gentleman's family,' Missus Hennessy, the midwife would have told her as she wrapped me in a shawl and placed me in my mother's arms. 'One girl and one boy.'

Mother would have smiled at the words, her mind focused on the noisy bundle at her breast.

'We better tell Tommy,' Missus Hennessy would have remembered. Mother would have liked to tell him herself but that was not how things were done then.

'Nothing will ever happen to ye as long as I live.' Mother's promise would have been whispered but no less solemn.

' 'Tis a boy, Tommy,' Missus Hennessy would have told Dad.

'Be the hokey,' he would have replied smiling, scratching the back of his head, half in wonderment, half in delight. And that would have been that.

A couple of minutes later he would have taken down the accordion and his foot would have stomped his excitement as he changed without pausing from Irish reels to Scottish strathspeys. Ma would have heard his music and understood his happiness.

My sister, Sam, would have gone to Granny Pey's so that she would be out of the way. The mystery of where babies came from would prevail to puberty and beyond. This was the right way of things.

Granny Pey was a heavy-set woman with a round, enquiring face and a high-pitched voice. 'What's up with ya, Sam?' she would have asked my sister as she stood in the middle of the stone floor near to the oilcloth-covered wooden table.

'What's out there in the wood, Granny?' Sam would have asked.

'What's that?' Granny would have strained to hear over the sizzling fire and the banging lid of the boiling pot of spuds.

'When I shout at the woods it shouts back,' Sam would have told her with amazement.

'Ahh, that's the headless son of the Woodcutter of Knockee Wood,' Granny would have explained. Her giggle would have heightened the mystery.

'You're pulling me leg, Granny.'

Granny Pey would have searched for her box of matches as dusk fell, lit the oil lamp and put the used match back in the box. The yellow light would have flooded the white-washed kitchen and blended with the silent dance of the flames from the fire. The patterned line of milk jugs would have shimmered on the dresser.

'How did he lose his head, Granny?' Sam would have asked, anxious to hear all the gory details but not really wanting to listen.

Granny Pey would have settled her bulk on one of the hobs under the chimney and Sam would have sat opposite her. 'One day a man called Jimmy Fagan was out cutting wood with his son, young Jimmy. He was one of the Fagan's of Ballindown,' she added. Sam would have nodded, even though she didn't know either the Fagans or Ballindown.

'Anyway, the old man had a fierce reputation. He would only ever say things once. He would never repeat himself.'

Sam would have strained forward and nodded. The sound of a lone car would be heard as it passed outside and granny would have peered through the small front window to see who it was. 'Well, be the hokey,' she would have continued, 'one day he brought young Jimmy with him into Knockee Wood over there and started to cut down a tree. "Timber!" he shouted, and the son didn't hear him. "What's that, Dad?" the son shouted back. But the old man never repeated himself.'

'So what happened, Granny?'

'The tree fell on young Jimmy and cut the head off him.'

Sam would have swallowed in disbelief.

'Aye,' Granny would have agreed. 'And the moral of the story is, young girl, you should always do what you're told the first time you're told to. So, off to bed with ya now or young Jimmy might decide to leave the woods and go on one of his visits. They say he's horrid mad on account of being without a head for so long,'

Granny would have laughed her high-pitched laugh that left Sam not knowing whether to believe her or not. That night Sam would have hugged the bedclothes—just in case!

And as evening gave way to night, Granny Pey would have lit the second oil lamp and turned on Radio Eircann to listen to Ceili House. She loved the chocolate box voice of MacMahuna. And she would have tapped her foot in time to the Gallowglass Ceili Band as they played 'Peter Street' and remembered the times when her whole family would gather round the fire of an evening and fill the place with the sounds of jigs, reels and ballads of far-off places. And then she would have made dough, placed it in a soot-covered griddle pan and the little house would have become cosy with the smell of baking bread. Then she would have knelt below the picture of Our Lady and asked Her and Her Son for forgiveness for her sins, secure in the knowledge that she must have sinned since such were the ways of humanity. Then she would have climbed to her lonely bed and slept the sleep of the unquestioning.

After all six of her brood were born, my mother would stand in the shop and boast about her accomplishments.

'What ages are they now?' Missus Fahey would enquire.

'Fifty, fifty-three, fifty-seven,' she would tell her and then pause for breath. 'Sixty, sixty-three, sixty-seven.' These were the years of our birth.

Birr

Summer 1958

Birr is a small and idyllic place bisected by the silver clear waters of the Camcor River and protected from the north winds by the gentle slopes of the Slieve Bloom mountains. To the west of the town, along the Athlone road lies the Bog of Allen; majestic strewn and home to a great variety of plants and animals. It occupies the heart of the Midlands of Ireland and that heart beats with a warmth and sense of irony that makes it a unique place and a place of much magic and wonderment for a young adventurist like me.

But my Birr was also a town of two churches. Saint Brendan's, the Catholic church, stands guard over a grey, granite bridge and the waterfall that urges the Camcor on its winding journey to the Shannon. But the Protestant church was also known as Saint Brendan's. It stood solemnly at the entrance to the tree-lined Oxmantown Mall and faced the closed, green gates of the castle, home to the Earl of Ross. No greater a testimony to irony could there be than that this land-locked town would name its churches after Saint Brendan the Voyager when the nearest seaport was nearly seventy miles away!

'It is a sin punishable by the fires of hell to set foot on that unconsecrated ground,' the Parish Priest told us in school. 'By the pains of hell!' he shouted.

And we believed him. But we always knew that the Protestant church wasn't all that bad on account of my best friend's mother being a Methodist and she was a very nice woman. And anyway, the Protestant church was run by Tom Mitchell, a happy, laughing man who dealt in our shop.

'If it's all right to take their money,' Ma told me, 'sure it can't be right to think of them as damned in hell. Sure what harm has poor auld Tom done to anyone?' I didn't know, but I wasn't going to risk my eternal soul to find out. So I asked God to quench my curiosity to see what the inside of the church was like.

Every day Tom would come to the shop and ask for 'a sliced pan and a quarter-pound of your best ham.' When I was there I used to duck behind the cash register in case he would put an evil eye on me and turn me into a Protestant. More than anything, I didn't want to see the inside of Old Nick's den.

'How come ya always ring the bell a minute before our lot?' Jimmy Whelan asked him one day. Jimmy was a small man with a pointy nose and playful blue eyes.

'Because our time is right and yours is wrong,' he laughed.

I asked Ma and she told me that the clock on the Protestant church was a minute fast but Tom Mitchell wouldn't give in. 'Why not?' says I.

'Who knows, son? But that's what happens when one side thinks they're better than the other.' Ma came from Northern Ireland, so she should know.

'Barney Robinson,' Sam once told me, 'is the fattest man in the whole world.' I believed her. 'D'ya know what he eats for dinner?' she went on.

'Whah?'

'A half-stone of spuds, three big chops, a whole head of cabbage and six pints of buttermilk.'

'Janey,' says I.

Every second day Barney would pant his way into the shop

and put his elbows on the counter. 'Give us a large bottle of lemonade, Missus Pey,' he would say.

'You get it,' Ma told me. I handed Barney the half-pint bottle of lemonade and he unscrewed the cap. I watched with wide eyes as he drank it down in one go, not pausing for breath; the air bubbles making the browny orange liquid froth in the bottle as it disappeared into his massive belly. Then he belched loudly in my direction and I smelt every dinner he had ever eaten. I vomited on the spot.

'God, ma'am,' says Barney, 'That lad seems to have a bit of a weak stumick. You'd want to bring him to the doctor. He isn't well.'

'Nothing to worry about. He's always been a bit weak in that area,' says Ma as she steadied me on my feet.

I told Sam about it later on and her nose screwed up in disgust. 'What did it smell like?' she asked.

'It was like something crept in and died in him,' says I.

Then John-Joe and Pak would arrive from the betting shop down the town. They lived with Barney in a small house down a winding, tree-lined lane. John-Joe was the educated one. He could figure bets in his head and always told me that 'when you're good at sums no fecker can do ya out of a shilling.' He would tap the side of his head with his index finger to emphasize the superiority of brainpower.

'Ya, har, yerrr,' Pak would say, backing up John-Joe's words of wisdom. John-Joe, Pak and Barney were like the three stooges. They went everywhere together. John-Joe was a dapper man who always wore a suit, badly washed shirt and a tie that was too small for him. He walked in front and would shout instructions to Pak, who walked three paces behind him. Pak would answer John-Joe in that guttural gibberish that only John-Joe understood. Barney would lag about five paces behind Pak, puffing and panting, trying to keep up.

My Dad used to say, 'I don't know what those three men would do without each other. Poor auld Pak would probably end up in the Portlaoise Asylum.' Portlaoise was home to the mental hospital for our area and no greater shame could befall a family than to have a member end up there. After that I felt sorry for him and I asked the Baby Jesus not to let me end up talking like Pak.

⸺

One Sunday afternoon Dad was sitting by the fire and listening to the match on the radio between Offaly and Tipperary. 'A great save by Ollie Walsh in the Offaly goalmouth,' Michael O'Heir screamed.

Dad dropped the *Sunday Independent* and shouted, 'Be the hokey fermer!' Sam and I clapped with glee. Ollie cleared the ball up the field and Dad picked up the paper. All was calm again. Then Dad started to laugh. 'Would ye look at the get-up of that,' he says.

'What's that,' says we. He showed us a photograph from the paper. It was a person in London with long, uncombed hair. It was wearing tight clothes. 'Is it a boy?' says I.

'Course it is,' says Sam. 'No woman would dress like that.'

'It's a beatnik,' says Dad and immediately roars with laughter.

'What's a beatnik?' Sam asks.

'It's a person that wants to look like Pak Fitzgerald,' says I.

⸺

Townsend Street was a continuation of the Athlone road and it started exactly one mile from the New Line and was landmarked by Alexander's Garage. The New Line got its name because twenty years earlier the council drew a continuous white line along the road right outside Missus Rafter's house.

Our shop and home lay halfway between Alexander's and the pillar that was once erected to the Duke of Cumberland but was rededicated to Robert Emmet after independence of the Irish Republic became a reality.

It was a small shop; its wooden shelves, made by John Corrigan, stacked high with the necessities of life and its Formica-topped serving counter faced with all the different brands of Jacobs biscuits: coconut creams, Mikado, fig rolls, and for the really adventurous, Afternoon Tea. Sam and me liked the Afternoon Tea the best and we would steal the chocolate-covered one with the piece of sugared jelly. Ma knew we were doing it but used to blame anonymous 'young scuts' when she was asked by customers where they were all gone.

From my earliest days I had a love-hate relationship with that shop. On the one hand I liked meeting the customers, full of advice, stories and often laden down with problems of just making ends meet in what were hard times. On the other hand I hated it and all the people who came there, because these stories and troubles kept our Ma away from me and there were so many things I wanted to tell her that I couldn't. When Ma's shift ended at seven in the evening, she was just too bushed to hear anything except happy stories from Sam and me.

Dad didn't get back from his job as a postman until nine at night, so either Sam or me had to mind the shop for two hours each day. This was another reason for cursing its existence. Once Dad got in he would put on his white shop coat and complete the transformation from postman to shopkeeper.

It seemed to Sam and me that all grown-ups ever did was to work and moan about their lot whilst thanking God for his blessings and all that. We didn't want to grow up and be cast in that role. It seemed as if the people we knew and loved thought of unhappiness with their lot as something God had visited on them so as to prepare them for the next, and better, life. Not to thank him for his misery, therefore, was to risk the even worse fate of everlasting damnation.

But music was our salvation. Every Sunday, after the match on the radio, the lads from the Marian Ceili Band crammed into our small kitchen and the shop would fill with customers who bought nothing. 'God blast it to hell,' one of them would shout when his tune was rejected by the group.

Then Dad would call things to order and pronounce final judgement. 'We'll play "The Rose of Tralee" followed by "The Flower of Sweet Strabane" and finish on "The Fields of Athenry". All in the key of D, lads.'

'Sounds better in E,' Uncle Timmy would chip in—just to raise the temperature a little.

'It makes the turn too hard,' Jimmy Grogan would say. His word was normally taken on account of the fiddle being the hardest instrument to play. Jimmy was tall, refined and looked like a musician from the Radio Eireann Symphony Orchestra.

Dad lifted his foot instead of a baton, hit the floor three times to give the beat, and the music started. It took a few bars for everyone to get in time. Then the music was as sweet as honey and you could feel the damp breeze on your face as you walked through the fields of Galway. Many a night I sat at the end of the stairs and drank the melodies, dreaming of flowing streams, tearful mothers, wild salmon and a history that found expression in the fingers of these men.

As the music changed from jigs to reels and finally to waltzes, Dad would pull funny faces from the strain of concentration, Uncle Timmy seemed as if he was somewhere else, Jim Grogan swayed with the undulations of the music and Micky Campbell, the drummer, would let out a few yelps as he laid into the drums. The customers in the shop responded to Micky's urges with yelps of 'Now you're knittin' it!'

Then I would get up and jump around as if I was Rory O'Connor, the great Irish dancer, and as if the music needed a purpose, the band would change key from D to E and the yelps of excitement blended with the tapping of the lid on the boiling kettle on the range. And the music would become more intense, their feet stomping the rhythm and me, the sweat pouring down my back, would eventually have to stop.

Then the music would come to an end and the musicians would applaud their expertise. The customers in the shop would yell for more. 'Be God, Tommy, your young lad will make a great dancer yet,' Jim Grogan said. His words were to be prophetic.

I started school when I was five, but because Auntie Bridie taught me how to write, I only spent four weeks in babies and low-first, and went straight to first class, completing three years of education in under one. I missed going to school earlier because I got jaundice and had to stay in bed for a long time and was not allowed to eat potatoes or sweets. I didn't miss the spuds!

Bang! You're Dead

By the time I was six I was given responsibilities in the shop. At first these were simple things like weighing potatoes, tea and sugar; cutting half-pounds of butter and sixpenny Ice creams or filling gallons and half-gallons of paraffin oil into cans for the customers who didn't have the electric yet. Pretty soon I was able to figure how many ounces in a pound, and I knew how many pounds were in a stone because Missus Barry only took a quarter-stone of new potatoes 'cos she lived on her own. Her husband died before I was born.

Every Saturday, around four o'clock, John-Joe would come into the shop. Pak and Barney would wait around the corner at Missus Cleary's wall because my mother hated the smell of drink off them and told them so.

'Any winners?' I would ask him.

'In God's world, my child,' John-Joe would say irreverently, 'we are all winners.' Even though John-Joe was officially a Protestant, he had no time for religion. He told me once that he only went to church at Christmas time and that he was so happy he wasn't a Catholic 'cos he could never tell his sins to the auld fecker of a Father Eamon.

I agreed silently and immediately asked for God to rid me of these unholy thoughts. 'Anyway,' I would say, 'I weighed in four hundredweight of potatoes belonging to Mister Rafter and we were paying one and six a stone. So that made four pounds eight shillings he got for his spuds.'

John-Joe would look at me and say, 'What age are ya?'

'Eight.'

'Well wouldn't ya think you'd have more sense.'

'But that was the right answer,' I would tell him.

19

'God, will I ever learn ya anything! Didn't ya know that auld Rafter always wet his spuds first and then threw clay on them. So you were paying good money for dirt!'

I hated being wrong. 'So what should I do?' I asked.

'Ya put the spuds on the scales and weigh them—just like before.' I nodded. 'Then ya tell him the weight. Just like ya did.'

'But ...' I said.

John-Joe put his fingers to his lips to command silence. 'Then ya say, "Mister Rafter, that was four hundredweight at one and six a stone. That's four pound even."'

'But that would be the wrong answer.' I protested.

'I know that,' John-Joe said, 'but auld Rafter doesn't. All he knows is that you paid him for his dirt!'

'But isn't that cheating?' says I.

'No, my son. That's show business!'

So I learned how to deduct ten percent from the purchase price of everything—just in case it had a bit of dirt thrown in—accidentally on purpose—and Rafter never seemed to mind!

'It's all about knowing the risk up front,' John-Joe continued, 'and then decidin' if it's worth it.'

'But how can you know that?' says I.

'Information, me lad. Information.'

John-Joe's theory was that if you studied everything about the horses you minimized the risk. 'Never bet on anythin' you don't understand,' he advised.

'Bleddy eejits, the lot of ye,' Barney concluded. 'Backin' horses is a mug's game. All the big races are fixed.'

'That might be so,' John-Joe agreed. 'But if ya know that ya can bet accordingly.'

'How would you know that?' I asked.

'By only riskin' yer money when you believe in the result. And so I learned the first rules of investment. Only put up your money when you know what you are investing in and only do so when you believe in the project.

The only time in the year that my mother would bet on a horse was on Grand National day. Either Sam or myself would open the shop and wait for Pak, John-Joe and Barney to arrive. On this day Mother tolerated the smell of stale Guinness and farmyard manure on Pak. 'Who'll win today, John-Joe?' she would ask.

'Ahh, grr, harr,' Pak would say as he broke into laughter.

John-Joe would look pensive, as if ready to deliver a Budget statement in the Dáil.

'Be gor, missus, I fancy the auld grey one meself.' Pak would heap scorn on this pronouncement.

'Are you backing him?' Mother would ask.

Barney would say how feckin' useless it was wastin' money like that on horses. 'Don't ya know, ya eejits, that it's only the bookie that makes money. Anyway, it's unpatriotic backin' an English horse when there's a couple of good Irish ones runnin'.' Pak appeared to agree with this.

'What would you know about it?' John-Joe spat, rounding on poor Pak. Pak's growl became more guttural.

'Mind he doesn't bite,' Barney laughs.

And Mother would settle on a horse and give John-Joe a pound. 'Ten bob, each way,' she would say. Then with John-Joe in the lead, Pak three paces behind mumbling obscenties and Barney waddling like a duck, they would make for the bookies in Main Street. Afterwards they would come back with the winnings and give it to my mother.

'What are odds?' I asked John-Joe.

'Odds, me dear man, are the bookies' calculations of the probability of that particular horse winnin' that particular race.' Pak agreed even though he was drunker than usual.

'Then it's easy,' I deduced. 'Just pick the one with the highest chance of winning.'

'It's not as simple as that,' John-Joe explained. 'Sometimes the bookie is wrong.' Pak gurgled and meant that this was a rare occurrence.

'And what happens when the bookie is wrong?' I asked.

'Then we win money,' John-Joe said.

'They're rarely bloody wrong,' Barney interjects. John-Joe ignored him. Pak, by this time, was in a lather of excitement and was becoming more boisterous by the minute.

Within a few months John-Joe had shown me how to calculate complex odds and to understand the nature of God's intervention in the outcome of horse races. In later years these simple calculations combined with the use of intuition were to become known as risk management. 'You see, young man,' he would say, 'it's just that auld Power the bookie is human so he's prone to make mistakes. Ya always have to keep an eye out for the margin of error. If ya keep one eye on this and the other on the form, you can work out if the risk is worth it.'

'And how do you know if the risk was worth it?' I asked.

'Ya only know when the race is over. Always remember that.'

Birr

June 1960

It was warm and the cattle in the fields chewed lazily on drying grass. Granny Pey had run out of stories and patience and was glad to get rid of Sam and me after looking after us for two weeks. Ma, she told us, was fine and we now had a new baby sister called Breda.

Sam and me got packed off to Granny Pey's but Dorothy, who was only three, got to stay at home. 'That's because she is too young to understand,' Sam complained.

'Understand what?' says I.

'How babies are made.'

'Any eejit knows that,' says I.

'Oh yeh. Well go on then smarty-pants.'

'Holy God creates them,' says I.

Sam laughs. 'Wrong,' she jeers.

'Well how then?'

'Did ya ever see a calf being born?'

'Of course I did.' I could remember one of Uncle Timmy's cows having a calf. 'They do attach a rope to it and pull because the cow was yellin' with pain.'

'That's how babies are born,' she says.

'Ya mean Missus Hennessy sticks a rope up Ma's arse and yanks on it,' says I with surprise.

'God, you're an awful eejit,' says she and walks off.

'Come back here ya little fecker,' I shouted after her. 'Ya have to tell me.' She never did.

Ma seemed really happy when we got home and we looked into the cot beside her bed at the little bundle that was to be our sister, Breda. 'You can mind her,' says Sam.

23

'You can bleddy mind her yerself,' says I.

'Shush,' says Ma, 'ya don't want the first words your little sister hears from your mouth to be a curse.'

'Bleddy is not a curse,' says I.

'It's not a nice word,' says Ma. I knew if she'd had more strength she would have given me a clip in the ear, so I didn't push my luck.

'I was thinkin',' says Ma, 'that we should go out and visit Aunt Lil. She's only ever seen photographs of ye. What do ye all say? What about next Sunday?'

'Does Dor have to come?' Sam asks.

'Of course,' Ma replies.

'Well Tom can mind her.'

'Bleddy well will not,' says I and Ma clipped my ear with the force of a Joe Lewis punch. Sam sniggered but I knew better than to retaliate.

The single-storey house at Coolfin was small and peaceful. Hens moved lazily in the hot sun, clucking gratefully as they pecked the cobble-strewn farmyard. A sow grunted its brood to suckle in the shade and a calf craved favour from the odd-looking strangers that came through the wrought-iron gate.

Dad locked the door to the old black Ford he had borrowed from John Corcoran, a local mechanic, and regretted having given into Ma who warned him against bringing his accordion along. 'I want the kids to meet Lil,' she told him, 'not to jump around like hooligans.' She knew that music had that effect on us.

Sam was dressed in a pink flowered frock and wore black patent shoes and white stockings. She complained from the time we left home that she looked like a banshee. Dor was dressed in a blue and cream frilly dress and Breda was dressed in a little pink number that had once been Dor's. I was dressed in brown knee-length corduroy trousers, a white shirt and a fawn, short-sleeved jumper set off with a red tie that was attached to my neck with elastic. My scuffed brown shoes were highly polished. Ma always took pride in how we looked but all we wanted to do was to explore the henhouse to find eggs. Ma read my mind and warned me off.

Aunt Lil was a tall, gangly woman with a narrow, weather-beaten face and a smile that lit up a room with warmth. 'Be God, is it yourselves?' says she as she rushed forward. Ma caught her hand and shook it. 'Come in, come in, let ye,' says Lil and we followed her into the small dark kitchen. Aunt Lil was wearing a long black dress that was covered by a flowered apron. 'Would ye like a cuppa tay?' she asks.

'You sit down there,' says Ma, 'and I'll get it.' Ma didn't want Lil to burn herself.

'Don't be frettin' over me,' Lil tells her. 'Just because I'm blind doesn't mean I'm handless.' There was no way that you could ever say that Lil O'Meara was the most decorative knife in the drawer but she was definitely one of the sharpest. She was born in the early 1890s and lived in the same house all her life. 'Things were different then,' she told us after Sam asked her if it was true that she was a hundred years old. 'Me father, Martin O'Meara, was a gamekeeper on the Burdett estate and he got this house and a few acres of land with the job.'

'It was a hard life,' Ma chipped in, 'for the lot of ye.'

'Be gorra it was,' says Lil. 'There was Mammy and Daddy and seven of us. Me brother, Martin, left home and became a gamekeeper up in Wicklow. Me two sisters went to America and never came back. Another brother became a station-master in Ferbane and got a fine house with the job. Him and I stayed on after me father died to look after me mother.'

'Hmm,' says Dad. He was a master of minimalism.

'But ya have a big farm now,' says Ma and added that God always rewarded the good.

'He does that,' says Lil, 'In the forties, the Land Commission divided up the Burdett estate and we got the house and fifty acres of land.'

'And then ya met Jim Egan,' says Ma.

'Aye. I did that,' agreed Lil.

'And he brought another eighty acres along with him.'

Lil giggled like a young girl. 'I suppose he had to bring something! He wasn't exactly a prize catch.'

'God, you're awful,' says Mother. But we all knew that Lil was only joking. She and Jim had no children but they looked after Kieran Egan after his parents died suddenly. Between the three of them they farmed their land. Jim was a great man with cattle and Lil made money from pigs, eggs and the best butter a man ever tasted.

Lil sighed and the conversation stopped. The tick-tock from the pendulum clock blended menacingly with the noise from the singing kettle on the black Stanley range. 'I'll make the tea then,' says Ma and she fished in her bag and took out a packet of Afternoon Tea.

'Watcha got there?' asks Lil.

'Afternoon Tea,' says I.

'Be the hokey,' says Lil as she pulled up a chair to the bare wooden table. 'We'll be the talk of the land.' Dad winced a little as he saw the profit from the shop being scoffed.

After tea, Aunt Lil brought me into her little garden to the rear of the house. The smoke from the chimney wafted past the flowering rhododendron and the bees busied themselves amongst the wild lavender.

'What ya can't see won't hurt ya,' Aunt Lil told me when I pointed out that the briars were choking her dahlias. 'They all smell just grand to me. And if God didn't want there to be briars they wouldn't grow.'

A small pet lamb came towards her, bleating for attention. She picked it up, cradled it in her arms and sat on a large stone that served as a garden seat. I sat on the ground and looked up at them both. Lil fumbled in her apron pocket and took out a baby bottle full of milk. The lamb suckled gratefully. 'Why are you doin' that?' I asked. Lil was too involved with the lamb to hear me. 'Aunt Lil,' I repeated, 'why are ya botherin' to feed it when it's only going to end up as a lump of mutton anyway?'

'A lump of mutton is a very useful thing,' she told me. 'You'll end up as boxed fertilizer if you're lucky. And if ya go to that place across the Irish Sea, could even end up in a vase and be no use to man nor beast.'

'Is it a boy or a girl?' I asked.

'It's a girl,' she replied. 'Lord save us, but don't they teach ya anythin' useful in that school of yours.'

'How can ya tell?' I asked.

'Just look at it under the moonlight. Ya need the moonlight all right.' Her roars of laughter were infectious and I joined in.

Aunt Lil's laughter subsided to silence and her attention went back to the suckling lamb that was drifting in and out of a trusting sleep. I, too, felt comfortable. It was as if this old woman was allowing me into her special place and was trusting me with her secret.

A frog jumped nearby and jumped again into the coolness

of the long, moist grass. 'Were you at Mass today?' she asked. 'What?' says I. She repeated herself. 'Ya.'

'So what did the priest have to say for himself then?'

'He was talking about coveting your neighbour's goods,' says I.

'Was he now?' The lamb moved in her arms and settled herself again.

'There, there,' she soothed. 'Ya don't covet anythin', now do ya?' The lamb didn't move from its comfort. 'So what did this priest have to say about covetin' then?' she continued.

'The priest said it was a sin to get jealous of someone else just because they had more than you.'

'Did he now. Did he now. And did he say anythin' about being jealous of someone just because they had less than you?'

'But why would ya be jealous of someone less well off than yourself?'

'Because it is easier for a camel to get through the eye of a needle than for a rich man to enter heaven.'

I was gobsmacked. I'd never though of that. 'That's stupid, Auntie Lil,' says I, 'sure nobody wants to be poor.'

'That's right, lad,' says she. 'Sure doesn't that show the great tomfoolery this religion is.' I looked bemused. I wasn't sure if it was a sin just to be listening to this sort of talk. But there was Aunt Lil, the lamb peaceful in her lap, sucking gratefully on the bottle of warm milk, and it all seemed so right. Anyway, if God didn't want us there we wouldn't be there. Just like the briars.

'It's simple,' she continued 'we all have souls that come from Himself and back there they'll go. And if He chooses you'll be rich then all the fightin' and covetin' in the world won't make ya poor. Nor, indeed, will all the prayin' in the world make ya any holier.'

She paused to resettle the lamb. 'Take this little lass for instance. The priest will have ya believe she has no soul. But does she not enjoy a nice sup of warm milk, just like anyone else?' I nodded. 'And if I beat her and taught her shoddy ways, would she not grow up to be an angry sheep; likely to kick the stuffin' out of ya if ya came near her?' I had to think about that one. 'Of course she would, lad,' she reassured me.

'But what does that mean?' I asked.

'It means that if we act the right way and don't teach people fear and anger then they'll be like the good lamb. Or we can teach people fear and that's the way they'll grow up.'

'I've lost ya,' says I.

'Look, lad. Take them priests. They'll tell ya that if ya do this and ya do that then you'll go to heaven.'

'Ya.'

'And they'll tell ya that if ya don't do this or that then you'll go to hell.'

'Ya.'

'So what do ya do?'

'I do what I'm told.'

'Right,' says Aunt Lil.

'But ...'

'But nothin', lad. You do what you're told because you're afraid of goin' to hell.'

'Of course,' I protested.

'So the only reason ya do it is out of fear. And because they tell you they're the only ones who will be saved on the Last Day, they teach ya not to love but to fear. So, Irishman fights Englishman, Catholic fights Protestant and the priests get fat. It seems to me like someone's got it all ass backwards.' She gently laid the lamb at her feet. It curled up in a satisfied ball.

'Aunt Lil?' says I. 'Do you go to Mass?'

'Be gub, I do,' says she.

'But …' says I with amazement.

'Like you, lad. I just want to be certain. Ya see lad, I'm probably more afraid than anyone and that's why I can talk about it.'

About three weeks later I told Ma what Aunt Lil had said. 'Don't be listening to her, son,' she warned me. 'Her and her crazy ideas.'

'Is it because she's blind that she says these things?' I asked.

'Who knows,' she tells me. 'All I can say is that you always have to live with your own conscience, so you should always do what you think is best. That's all God can ask of anyone.' Ma's advice made me no more the wiser but Aunt Lil's words were to revisit me later in my life. It was then that I understood what both she and Ma were telling me.

It was hot and humid after the summer rain. School was out about a month when my friend Jimmy called for me to go out and play. 'Bring Bonzo,' he told me. Bonzo, was a collie cross but once out playing with us he became Rin-Tin-Tin.

'Go get 'em,' I would shout, then slapping my thigh to the rhythm of a galloping horse I followed the dog on my imaginary steed as the Seventh Cavalry came to the rescue of a wagon train trapped by marauding Indians.

'Bang! You're dead,' Jimmy shouted as he appeared from behind a tree.

I lay on the wet grass, counted to twenty a little faster than

I was supposed to, then rose from the dead, mounted my horse again and ordered the imaginary platoon to follow me. 'Yoh–ho–o,' I would shout, throwing my right hand in the air and pointing in the direction of the Comanches.

Our back garden was the best place in the world for gun-fights. The trenches my father dug for potatoes saw some of the fiercest fighting of the Second World War, and the peas hid the merry band of Robin Hood's men from the dreaded clutches of the Sheriff of Nottingham. The pampas grass that was never given a chance to show its splendour, provided Robin with a supply of arrows.

To the back of our shed stood a lone sycamore. Many a time I hid among its leafy branches, selecting a long, straight stick that would convert to a bow. The roof provided a spot where the Cisco Kid could run along its apex, gun drawn, slouched lest the gangsters would see him. Then the Kid would jump from the gable end into the pit, which was filled with cardboard boxes from the shop, and escape to fight another day.

In the evenings we would light the boxes in the pit and me and Jimmy would dance around the flames calling on the spirits to make us fearless in battle. 'I want to be the Kid,' Jimmy insisted.

'No me,' I retorted.

'You can't be the Kid. The Kid never had a dog.'

I was stumped. 'Okay. You're the Kid and I'm Captain Browne from Fort Worth. You are accused of robbin' a bank and I have to bring you in. Rinnie is my scout dog.'

'But when I'm tried I'll be found not guilty. Okay?'

I agreed. Then Jimmy, the Kid, sped off on his horse, round the back of the shed and hid in the sycamore. I counted to a hundred and ordered Rin-Tin-Tin to begin the chase.

Rin-Tin-Tin was no fool. He could smell the Kid a mile away. 'Bang! Bang!' the Kid shouted.

'It's no use Cisco,' Captain Browne shouted back as he began shooting. 'It's no use Rinnie,' Captain Browne tells the dog. 'We need to get behind him.' The dog took off and evaded all the bullets from the Cisco Kid's gun. 'That's six shots, Kid,' Captain Browne shouts. 'You're outa bullets. Come out with yer hands up and I'll see to it you get a fair trial.'

The Cisco Kid scorned the offer. 'You think I came to this place without having a stash of ammo, eh?'

'Damn,' I swore, 'I hadn't figured on that. I'm going back to Fort Worth. But I'll be back with more men.' Captain Browne never minded about lying to crooks. He mounted his horse slowly and deliberately. Then he slapped his thighs and the horse took off as the Kid scorned his retreat.

Down in the yard, Captain Browne found a ladder. He placed it against the front side of the shed and crept along the roof to the apex. The Kid didn't hear a thing. Then Rin-Tin-Tin gave the game away. He had climbed up the ladder and scrambled along the roof to the apex, and just when Captain Browne was about to plug the Kid in the back, he barked. The Kid turned with the agility of a snake. 'Bang! You're dead,' he shouted.

I clutched my breast and fell forward. I slipped on the roof and fell through the sycamore and banged my nose on the branches on the way down. The blood spurted everywhere and Cap'n Browne could be heard screaming in America. Ma rushed from the shop and picked me up. 'Would ya look at the cut o' ya,' she scorned. 'Get yourself inside till I take a look.' But the bleeding wouldn't stop and I was taken to the doctor. He put a lump of cotton wool or something up my nose and told me not to play cowboys for a couple of days. I nodded.

About four weeks later my mother noticed a black streak under my eye. 'What's that Bridie?' she asked my aunt. Bridie was a nurse and our resident medical expert.

'That's blood poisoning,' says she. 'Get him down to the doctor's quick.' Off we went to the surgery for the second time. 'He's been sniffin' a lot lately,' Ma told the doctor, 'and now he's got this black mark.'

The Doc shone a light up my nose and told me I would have to be a brave lad. 'You got a slug o' whisky, Doc?' says I.

'Mother o' God,' Ma says, 'you'd think we were drinkers or somethin'.'

'No whisky lad. But I could come up with the price of an ice-pop if you don't scream.'

'Deal,' says I.

The removal of the piece of sycamore bark from my nose didn't hurt but I pretended it did. The Doctor gave me the price of an ice-pop and Ma gave me a small bar of Cadbury's Dairy Milk when we got home. I gave Rin-Tin-Tin a little bit of the chocolate. 'In future,' I told him, 'you only move on my command. Understand?' The dog lay his head on my lap and I scratched the back of his ear. 'Oh, okay then,' says I. 'I guess one mistake is okay.'

Birr

June 1963

It was coming close to the summer holidays from school and the farmers were already praying for rain. We weren't. All we wanted was for the sunshine to continue so that we could go to Sandymount and swim, so Jimmy and me decided to pray harder than the farmers.

Each evening, after school, I would do my homework and Auntie Bridie, who was living with us for a couple of years, would correct my mistakes. She was a tall, handsome woman with a soft Northern Irish accent. This meant she used the word 'och' a lot when I did something stupid or smart. 'Och, but aren't you the clever one,' she would say, and Sam would stick her tongue out at me in envy.

The house at Townsend Street served three functions. Firstly, it was our home and since Ma was pregnant again it was about to house eight of us—Ma, Da, Sam, me, Dorothy, Breda, Tony, Auntie Bridie and the new baby.

'I think it's disgustin',' Sam told me one day as we sat in the garden.

'What is?' says I.

'Ya know. Mammy and Daddy!'

'What?'

'Ah you're feckin' stupid?' she spat.

It also housed our shop. Most of the customers had dealt with us for years and they would buy their groceries 'on the book' and pay for them at the end of the week. They dealt with us because they liked Ma and because they felt they were helping a decent family to get on. This, above all else, is my abiding memory of the Irish sense of fair play.

In the evening, however, around half past nine the house

became a vestibule for passing musicians. Its walls would reverberate to the sweet, melodic tones of Irish jigs and reels and we tapped our feet to the lovely hornpipes with their hidden promises of lazy days on board sailing ships just off Galway Bay.

And when they came to a turn in the music, Dad would lift his eyebrows and bounce his accordion rhythmically and, like obedient schoolboys, the musicians would change to a new tune. Now and again one of them would miss the turn and the rest would prevail with the ensuing cacophony.

'When I was a young one,' Ma told me, 'I would spend hours at the crossroads dancing the night away.'

'And what time would ya get home?' I enquired.

'I'd be in Paddy Kelly's yard by cockcrow and be ready to get on with the day's milkin' or whatever had to be done.' I wondered what she would say if I was to stay out all night.

On that night Ma doubled over and all the musicians stopped playing and left. 'Best of luck, missus,' they said, and Dad looked concerned.

'I'd better get Missus Hennessy,' says he. Mother nodded and he helped her to bed. Aunt Bridie took all of us children out to Granny Pey's and we sat up all night playing snap and listening to stories. Granny Pey was great at telling stories. She could scare the livin' daylights out of you with that high-pitched giggle. Anyway, Sam was afraid of ghosts and wouldn't let any of us go to sleep lest the headless coach came on its way to the castle and took us away with it.

'What'd happen, if ya got inside the coach?' I asked Granny.

'Oh ho, be gor now. You wouldn't come back.'

'And where would ya go?' I asked.

'Straight to the hobs of hell, lad. Straight to Auld Nick himself.'

Sam crossed herself and Dor started to cry, even though she didn't know who Auld Nick was. A log moved in the fireplace and we sat in silence listening to Jimmy Shand and his ceili band on the gramophone. And we thought of far-off places as beautiful as the Lakes of Killarney and of Ma and Da and our little house in Townsend Street.

The next day we were introduced to the last member of our family. He was named after St Brendan the Navigator. 'Where did our little brother Brendan come from?' I asked.

'The stork brought him,' Da told us. Sam scoffed in disbelief and I was confused. Within a couple of weeks the music started up again and Brendan slept to the rhythm of stomping feet.

'When I was a young one,' Mother told me, 'I used to go to the Feiseanna.'

'What are they, Ma?' says I.

'That's where Irish talent go to compete and see who's the best.'

'And what were you the best at?' Sam asked.

'I was a great one at reciting Irish poetry. You see, my father was a gamekeeper at Cloghan Castle but on account of his getting mixed up with the IRA he had to go on the run.'

'What did he do?' I asked. I had visions of Grandad O'Meara being like Ned Kelly, the famous Australian bandit who robbed the English and gave the money to poor people.

'Ah, I don't know. Nothin' much, I think. But he spent a little time in Tullamore Jail.'

'Janey,' we all said in admiration.

'Ah, he didn't like the Tans and he thought he'd do something about it, I suppose,' Ma offered in mitigation. 'Anyway,' she continued, 'when the troubles were over, Grandad moved to Northern Ireland and I stayed behind with the Kellys in Lusmagh.'

'Was he on the run, Ma?' I asked.

'Lord no, son. Sure if he was on the run he'd hardly move to English territory, now would he?' I was disappointed. 'I went to school in Banagher and learned to speak fluent Gaelic. So when I moved up North I was the last Irish speaker in the land.'

'Why? Do they not speak Irish up there?' Sam asked.

'You're shockin' stupid,' says I. 'Sure isn't that part of England?'

'It's part of Ireland too, smarty pants,' she retorted.

'Stop arguing,' Ma snapped. 'So, I used to go to the Feiseanna and compete. I won a load of medals.' She smiled with pride and moved the boiling kettle to a cooler part of the range to stop the lid from banging. 'But I used to spend hours sitting under the stage looking at the Irish dancers and I'd cry all the way home because we were too poor for me to learn. But I swore my kids would get the chance.'

The next Tuesday Sam, me and Ma went to meet Missus Cunniffe, the Irish dancing teacher. She was a small, round-faced woman with a wide smile and an expensive hairdo. When she danced her enormous breasts hopped up and down. 'One of these days,' I told Sam, 'if she's not careful, she'll take yer eye out with them things.'

'Them things are called bosoms,' she smirked, 'and you're only jealous 'cos boys can't have them.'

'Sure what use are they?'

'They're for feeding babies,' says Sam.

'You're kiddin',' says I. But she assured me she knew what she was talking about.

Dad and the other musicians who used to play in our kitchen made up the Marian Ceili Band. The band was christened following the announcement by the Catholic Church that Our Lady was assumed body and soul into heaven. That was on the ninth of December 1950. Sam was born on the twelfth of December of that year and this ex- plains the origin of her name. The Marian bit had to do with it being declared the Marian Year. 'Give it "Haste to the Weddin' " in D,' Dad would tell them and they would blast the hell out of it.

'Get up there and give us a bit of a dance,' Ma would tell us. We would complain but the musicians would have none of it. Up we would get and do our hop one, two, three. Hop one, two, three, and the music would get sweeter and be played with more purpose. And one of them would give a yell and the intensity of feeling in the playing would rise to near fever pitch as the sweat poured off them and us.

When they finished they would clap one another and say, 'God, ye'll make fine dancers, the pair of ye.' And as they would go home, they would say 'Thanks Missus' to my mother as they mopped their brows with their crumpled handkerchiefs.

I just loved the music. I could feel its rhythm pulsate in my veins and I would conjure up images of great horse races or mischievous fairies and I could travel outside myself to far-off places. I loved to dance to it and to try to express what I felt and saw but never quite managed to get others to understand what was inside of me. I feel the same way today. For me there is no music as magical as Irish music and no musicians as mystical as those who played in our kitchen. Their tunes will remain a part of me forever.

After a couple of years practising and going to Feiseanna every Sunday, Da thought it was time I shared my talent for dancing with the general public. Both Da and my Uncle Timmy (who was one of the musicians in the Marian Ceili Band) had formed a branch of Ceolthas Cheoltoiri Eireann, a national organisation set up to promote traditional Irish culture. The branch was now run by their second cousin, Paddy Duffy.

Paddy used to arrange concerts and Da thought it would be a good idea if I danced and he played for me—a sort of double act. Paddy agreed and so started my stage career. 'Always leave the stage, a mhic,' Da would say, 'when they're clappin' for more.' I knew what he meant but Da didn't. I'd be winded after two dances and the crowd would be shouting 'More! More!'

'Do it yourselves, smart-arses,' I would mumble as I bowed humbly and smiled. Da never looked like he would leave the stage.

One night, however, I saw Kathleen Watkins play the Chualainn at a posh concert in Dublin. She was such a marvellous player that you didn't know whether to hug her or cry. But anyway, when she was finished, the crowd were on their feet shouting for more. All she did, as cool as a gooseberry, was to bow politely and then wave her arm in the direction of the orchestra that was playing for her. They stood up, the audience went mad and she fecked off the stage without having to play any more.

After that I was always able to keep to Da's rule and leave the stage before I got something thrown at me. I would turn to Da and give him the nod. This was the signal I was coming to an end of the dance at the end of that bar of music. We would stop. The crowd would roar for more. I would bow politely and then, with a wave of my arm, invite Da to share in the adulation. The crowd would go mad, Da would settle down for an encore and I would feck off the stage leaving them clapping for more. I knew Da was mad at me but at least the stitches in my side stopped.

My Dad was a man of few words but never failed to express himself in his music. He had a way of playing that made you feel that each note was being played especially for you. I used to sit for hours listening to him playing. His notes were sweet and they touched a place inside me that fired my imagination. I experienced the freedom of walking across distant hills with 'The Boys of the Blue Hill', heard the clatter of hooves on softened turf and then the momentary silence as the horses arched gracefully over fences as their cursing jockeys urged them to win 'The Kilkenny Races', and visited the sorrows of the exiled as they struggled to conjure images of 'Spancell Hill' or the stony wilderness of 'Crees Lough' in County Donegal.

And as I learned to dance I began to hear every note form and linger, and the pictures changed from dreams to a reality that needed to be expressed. 'Be gor,' Jimmy McLaughlin, a customer in the shop, told Ma once, 'but that young lad of yours is a powerful dancer. Ya know, if ya close yer eyes you'd think you were up there on the stage with him. He says things with his feet most men can't say with their mouth.' Ma would flush with pride. But Da and I knew the real secret. We had touched one another's souls in a way that transcended words or deeds. We shared one another's art and became acquainted with the very spirit that made us both what we were.

I feel honoured to have known my father as deeply as so few do.

Birr

Autumn 1963

There was about a week to go before we were due to go back to school and the gang of us, who usually hung around together, decided to have a last big stone fight with the lads from Oxmantown Mall. So, Jimmy, Monk, Pon, David and me met with Candle Walkins and we went off to the riverside to fill our pockets with stones. Candle Walkins was really Johnny McGee and he got his name because his nose was permanently running and he sniffed a lot. My friend, Jimmy, told him one day that he produced enough snot to start a candle factory and the name stuck.

Just down from the waterfall the water bubbled over stones and along its frothy banks was a clump of trees that served as our headquarters. We met there any time we wanted to have a council of war and today we wanted to teach the bozos from the Mall a lesson.

'No surrender,' we pledged, as Pon, who was the eldest, told Jimmy and me that we would have to ride point. What this really meant was that we would have to go along the Mall and shout names at the Mall lads and when they got mad and ran after us we were to hightail it back towards Townsend Street, where the rest of the gang lay in ambush. 'You lads are picked for this special duty,' says Pon, 'because you are the best runners.' Off we went, past the Protestant church and deep into enemy territory.

'Cissy Mallissy,' shouts me at Donal Brick, the biggest lad on the Mall. He ignored me.

'Brickie kissed Mary Johnson,' says Jimmy. Nobody wanted to kiss poor Mary. Monk said she was as ugly as Poll Ashe that died of shame, and we agreed.

That did it. Brickie shouted the war cry of the Mall lads and they appeared out of nowhere. Jimmy and me ran like divils and now and again I heard the wind of stones as they shot past my ear. Then, for no reason it stopped and the Mall lads weren't following us anymore.

'Cowardy, cowardy custard,' shouts me, 'stick yer nose in mustard.' But the Mall lads were interested in something else. Jimmy and me approached them cautiously. They didn't seem to care. Finally, we went up to them. 'What's wrong?' says I.

'Shhh,' says Brickie, 'I think it's a weasel,' as he padded the undergrowth with a piece of stick. We all crouched expectantly. Just when we were about to give up, out shoots the weasel and makes his way down the Mall towards Townsend Street.

'Get the bastard,' shouts Brickie and we all took off after the weasel that was running in the direction of the Townsend Street Gang. They saw us coming and prepared to pelt us with stones but we all shouted for them to get the bloody weasel and they joined in the chase. About ten of us chased the weasel along Townsend Street and back up Glebe Street until it finally went down into Missus O'Hare's basement.

'Get a feckin' box,' Pon commands, and I raced back to our shop and returned with a big cardboard box.

'Right,' says Brickie, 'I'll go down and get the weasel. Here and don't let him escape.' Brickie climbed down into the basement and the weasel backed himself into a corner.

'Mind he doesn't go for your throat,' Pon warns. It was a well-known fact amongst all gang members that if a rat was trapped in a corner it would jump and bite your throat in order to get away. Brickie tucked in his chin like a boxer.

Brickie eyed the weasel, the weasel eyed Brickie and we

remained silent. Then, with the agility of a safari hunter, Brickie rams the box over the weasel. We cheered with delight.

'You feckin' eejits,' says Pon. 'What good is that?'

'Watcha mean?' says I.

'The bleddy weasel is in the box. How do we close the box?'

'Easy,' says Brickie and he puts his hand under the box to catch the weasel.

He withdrew it almost immediately and started to cry. 'The fecker bit me,' he cried. Just then the weasel decided he had enough of the game and he came out from behind the box. With the respect he had earned from biting Brickie he ran up the wall, across the railings and was out of our trap before we could say Jack Smith.

We brought Brickie to the Doctor, who made us all tell him what had happened. 'You're all lucky lads,' he tells us. 'He could have taken young Brick's finger off with one chop.'

'Will he die?' I asked.

'You got him here on time,' the Doctor told us. 'I'll have to give him an injection though.' We all turned our backs as the Doc rolled up Brickie's sleeve. Then we heard Brickie scream and we wanted to run away. Candle Walkins nearly fainted because he hated to think of blood. After surgery we held a council of peace and we vowed never to fight one another again—until next summer at least.

Even though it meant going back to school, I always loved the first stages of autumn. I would take our dog and walk through the fields, the wind and rain in my face, and try to figure out where on the map of the world the horizon fell. Wherever that was I wanted to visit.

To the north I figured it had to be the North Pole with its white ice, blizzards and polar bears. To the south it had to be the South Seas and promise of buried treasure. To the west the sky just touched America with its wide open plains, police sirens and the honking horns of New York. I never wanted to go east because the Commies lived over there and the priests always told us that the Commies were 'evil blackguards' sent on Earth by the Devil himself to rob Catholic souls. I wanted to keep mine thank you very much.

But I loved being alone around this time each year because it gave you a chance to think about the things that were important. The wind whipped through the chestnut trees that lined the Rector's wall in Glebe Street, just behind our house. I walked through the brown fallen leaves and felt the crunching texture beneath my feet. The trees made a lonely sound and I could hear in them the slow airs and solemn marching music of old Ireland and I would scrape my feet in time to its monotonous beat. But every now and then I would hear jigs and reels and I would tap the merriment on the dying carpet and feel safe being alone with the elements. Nature, I realized, was something that was bigger than myself.

I began collecting the leaves and placing them in a mound, intent on building a comfortable place where I could just sit alone and be with me. Building the place just seemed to be an important thing to do. Then I sat there with my eyes closed and I saw a little boy sitting on a stone. His back was towards me but I knew from the short hair and sticking-out ears that it was me. Beside him sat a figure in the form of a white cloud, his arms around me as we both stared into a bluey brightness.

'What will I do when I grow up?' I thought.

'You will do something that makes a difference,' the answer came back.

'Will I be rich?' I asked. No answer.

'What will I be?' I insisted.

'You will learn to believe that you are a good person,' the voice replied. I didn't know what it meant then but my eyes filled with tears anyway. Being a good person seemed enough for me at the time.

Ma was reading the paper and I was studying up the Beano. 'Would you look at the get-up of these,' she chuckled. Sam, who was suffering from teenagerism, tried not to be interested. I was still of an age where I appreciated a good laugh. We looked at the photograph in the *Irish Independent*.

'Honestly,' Sam declared. 'That's the Beatles.'

'Beatles!' Mother shouted in disbelief. 'It's a good name for them alright. Wouldn't ya think their mothers would have made sure they had a decent haircut before they let them out? God, wouldn't you be just scared if you met them in a dark alley?'

'They only happen to be the best group in the world,' my sister informed us. Mother turned the page and began reading about Doctor Noel Browne's latest capers in the Dáil and I went back to my comic.

'Do you want to hear my new transistor radio?' Sam asked.

'Yeah,' I replied enthusiastically.

She turned it on to Radio Luxembourg and Kid Jensen faded in and out as the signal eddied, but we could make out the sound of the Beatles singing 'From Me to You'. Sam gyrated to the rhythm.

'You don't have the moves,' she told me as I tried to imitate her.

'Watcha mean?'

'You have to be in the groove to move,' she told me as she waddled like a duck and flapped her arms around like a lapwing.

'Call that music,' Ma screamed above the din. 'Janey Mac, what is the world coming to at all? Wouldn't ya be better off practising your Irish dancing?'

'Boring,' sis insisted without pausing for breath. I was fed up and could see no point gyrating like a crazed Pawnee. Then Kid Jensen introduced Billy Fury singing 'Halfway to Paradise'.

'At least you could listen to that,' Ma declared 'not like those other insects, whatever ya call them.'

Sam was in a world of her own doing a bad impression of a dying swan. Billy kept on singing like he really knew what was going on in our kitchen. But the Philips transistor radio, huge by today's standards, was her link to a world that was preparing for a cultural revolution. She meant to be part of it, but that fear Aunt Lil talked about stopped her. That fear was to stop a lot of people.

'D'ya know what?' says I.

'What?' says Sam.

'O'Hagan's got a new car and it has a transistor in it.'

'Watcha mean?' says Sam disbelievingly.

'It's built into the car. Near the steering wheel,' says I.

'How do you know?'

' 'Cos Jimmy showed it to me.'

'Did you hear it?'

'No, 'cos you have to turn on the engine first.'

'What'll they think of next?' Ma sighed. The world was changing too fast for her, but around that time I began to see the future as an adventure. This was a feeling that was to remain with me up to today—except for a short period when I experienced Aunt Lil's fear.

Slowly but surely the foot-stomping musicians stopped coming to the house in the evenings, their brand of music no longer in vogue. Then the evenings were silent except for the crackling Radio 208 and the new language of youth. But Dad and me continued to be an item on the stages of Ireland.

Birr

June 1965

'Do you know,' Aunt Lil said, 'I think this pop music was sent on Earth by the Devil himself just to torment us.'

'It's not that bad, Aunt Lil,' says I, 'ya get used to it.'

'God knows how,' she declared. 'Sure it'd drive the beasts from the fields.'

'And what about in your time?' I asked.

The old woman's greyed eyes seemed to fill with light. 'I was a divil,' she admitted. 'I would sneak out at night and walk miles to an auld dance at some crossroads or other.'

'Ya mean in the open air.'

'Be gor aye. We'd dance under the stars till the cows would come home. Then we'd find a chap with a bike to bring us home.' She giggled like a young girl.

'And what sort of music did they play?'

'The finest of Irish tunes. Them were the days, young lad. Innocent and full of fun.'

'And what would happen if it rained?' I asked.

'The summers then were far better than now,' she declared. 'Anyway, what harm is a drop of rain? All we'd do is stand under a tree till it passed. But the musicians would play on and on, and every now and again someone would give us a song.' Aunt Lil blew her nose and turned her back so that I wouldn't see her tear of reminiscence. For the first time I came to realize that Aunt Lil was once a young girl, full of fun and a zest for life, with eyes that could see.

'When was that, Aunt Lil?' I asked after a few moments.

'When was what?' she snapped.

'The crossroad dances. What year was that?'

'Oh God, it's so long ago I can't remember. I started going

to them in 1910. I was about sixteen then and only a whip of a thing. But I really got going in 1918.'

'That was the time of the Black 'n Tans,' says I.

'The bloody blackguards,' she sighed. 'They put paid to a lot of things ya know. Aye be gor.'

'Like what?'

'Poor auld Johnny Meara, God rest his soul, held great house dances. People came from miles around for his parties. His wife, Maggie, would make seven or eight big cakes of soda bread and lash them with home-made country butter. God, they were gorgeous. Anyway, Johnny had an auld gramophone. Ya know the wans ya wind up. And people used to give him seventy-eights of Irish dance music.'

She blew her nose again. 'One evening we were having a great time. The fire was blazing in the hob. Maggie was fillin' out cups of tay, shoutin' at everyone to mind themselves lest they got scalded. Then the Tans came.'

'What did they look like?' I asked.

'Like the blackguards they were, lad. Bloody blackguards.'

'And what happened then?'

'Auld Johnny stopped windin' and the music got slower and slower. We were all frightened. Then one of the soldiers said we were all Fenian bastards. He was drunk. He kept sayin' he hated Fenian bastards. Then Johnny got up and offered them a cup o' tay. The mouthy lad hit him across the side of the head with the butt of his gun and then smashed the gramophone into smithereens.'

'And did none of the lads try to stop them?' I asked.

'No. They just looked on and their hatred grew inside them. But they said nothin'. You see, young lad, if ya gave them any auld lip they'd be likely to shoot. They didn't care. Look what they did in Croke Park.' Every Irishman knew the story of Croke Park when the footballers in the All-Ireland final were shot by the Tans.

'So did they go away?'

'Aye lad. They left all right. But first they made each of the girls dance with them. Then they took all of Maggie's hens.'

'God,' says I, 'I'd lose me temper with them.'

'No, lad. Remember that no matter what happens you have to accept that things are today exactly as they should be. That was our motto anyway.'

'Ah come on, Aunt Lil,' says I. 'Surely the Tans ...'

'The Tans made us a strong nation,' Aunt Lil told me. 'Ireland got its independence shortly after and as soon as it did the music started again. And the people were poor but helped one another. We were all friends. That wouldn't have happened if we didn't have to endure the Tans.'

'And what about Johnny Meara?'

'He never held a house dance again,' she replied.

'Why was that?' I asked.

'Because he went deaf, lad. The blow to his head damaged his good ear. He never heard again. And let that be a lesson to ya, lad. No matter what happens to ya, never hold hatred in yer heart for another man. It'll only poison ya.' Every time after that, when I heard the Lord's Prayer, I knew what it meant.

Birr

Summer 1966

'A man who forgets where he came from has no past,' John-Joe told me one Saturday after he had a couple of pints too many. 'And a man who has no past has no future,' he prophesized.

'Sure, John-Joe,' says I, 'but shouldn't you be getting home?'

John-Joe swayed a little but looked at me intently. He steadied himself like a man at the bow of a ship in a swell. 'Promise me you won't forget this street, its people, this aul' shop, me ...'

'I promise.'

'If ya keep that promise, young lad, you'll go places. Mark my words.'

But it was 1968, Radio Luxembourg played the type of music my parents hated even more than before, I got my first pair of hipsters and my first taste of politics. The whole world seemed to be changing all at once.

Eamon De Valera, who had controlled the Irish body politic since the birth of God's dog, was running for president against T.F. O'Higgins, the son of a former co-conspirator who was later a supporter of Michael Collins. Ireland was evenly divided along civil war lines for what was to be the last time. O'Higgins hoped to overthrow the king, and Tommy Pey, together with the rest of the Fine Gael party, was going to make sure it happened!

'Don't vote for Dev,' I roared across the microphone. My voice boomed through the speaker mounted on top of Micky Madden's mini van. 'He had a chance to die for his country,' I accused. 'But what did he do?' Willie Smith, a grey-haired

Englishman who drove for Micky wasn't too comfortable with my line of attack. He winced. 'He told the Brits he was a bleddy American citizen,' I disclosed. 'Vote O'Higgins. Vote for an Irishman proud of his heritage.'

We lost and Dev won. But with a reduced majority thanks to my disclosures, and O'Higgins went on to become Chief Justice of the Supreme Court. He never came looking to thank me, and calumny remained no sin in youthful pursuit of political change in Ireland.

Another opportunity for using my oratorical prowess came when Liam Cosgrave decided it was time to get rid of the Fianna Fáil lackies (supporters of Dev) and get some real men into the Dáil. Tom Enright, a young local solicitor decided to throw his hat in the ring and I was ready, willing and able to help. This time we won.

Tom became a Member of Parliament (TD) and Richie Ryan became Minister for Finance. Everything went well for about twelve months and then all hell broke loose in our house.

My father and mother were Fianna Fáil to the core, but had given their first preference vote to Tom Enright on account of his being a fine lad and from the town. Now they rued the day they had ever allowed their son to influence a shift in their loyalties. 'Feck it to hell,' Dad roared when he read the headlines in the *Evening Press*: RICHIE BRINGS IN WEALTH TAX, it bellowed.

'Now look at what that auld bags has done,' he shouted at me with the pain of the tortured. 'We'll all be ruined.'

'Richie Ryan, me hat,' Ma chirped in. 'More like Richie Ruin if you ask me.'

'We need economic stability,' I told them. 'The country was left in an awful state by the last lot.'

'Economic stability!' My father was barely able to contain himself.

'We'll all be ruined. Feckin' income tax and now this.'

My undying loyalty remained. I didn't waver in the face of such hostility. 'Sacrifice,' I told them, 'is good for the soul.' Neither of them spoke to me for three days.

The coalition between Fine Gael and Labour and the stewardship of Liam Cosgrave were not to be blessed with the longevity normally expected of an Irish government. After four and a bit years they were out on their ears and I was supporting them in opposition once more.

Jim Cashin was a great flute player and he used to play at some concerts where Da and I were performing. 'Be gub,' people would tell him, 'but that's the best "Old Bog Road" we ever heard. Sure you'd think you were in New York itself.'

'Be God, thanks Missus,' Jim would say. And then he would turn to me and say, 'Ya need to keep the feckers sweet, young lad.' I told Aunt Lil about Jim.

'If they only knew the truth,' Aunt Lil told me. 'Sure isn't Broadway the place where all them film stars and the like perform on stage?'

'I don't know, Aunt Lil,' says I, 'but I intend to go there one day.'

'They say it's a grand place, New York.'

'I've seen it on telly,' says I. 'There's lots of motor cars and buses and crooks.'

'God be with them,' she prays, crossing herself, 'surely

not in such a grand place. Anyway I'm sure they have the Garda just like here.'

'They have,' says I, 'only they call them cops.'

Silence.

'I saw a photograph of it once,' Aunt Lil says.

'Of what?'

'Of New York—Times Square. They say it's near Broadway.'

'You could see?' says I.

'Oh, I saw enough. I saw the Tans come and go, and that lovely man, Padraig Pearse—before they shot him.'

'When was that, Aunt Lil?'

'I saw Pearse in 1912. He and Collins stayed near here for a couple of nights and we went down and had a cup of tea with him. He was a fine-looking man. He had learnin'. Knew lots of poetry.'

'And then he died for Ireland,' says I.

'Be God, he did.' says she with pride.

Silence.

'Have a drop of lemonade, young fella,' Aunt Lil said.

'Thanks,' says I. I hated her lemonade. It was always old and flat because she kept half-full bottles for years rather than throw them out.

'And then you can sing a song for me,' she adds.

' "A Nation Once Again", Aunt Lil?' says I with the same pride as she shared when she talked about Pearse.

'Aye, son. A grand song.' Aunt Lil poured the lemonade into a cup. Not only was it flat but it was a funny colour as well. It looked like water. Maybe somebody got fed up drinking her flat lemonade so they threw it away without her knowing and replaced it with water. There was nothing for it but to down it in one.

I did. Nothing happened for a few seconds then my chest

hurt. I thought it was going to explode. Then my eyes started to water and I couldn't stop coughing. 'What the heck's wrong with ya, young lad?' says Aunt Lil.

I couldn't talk. 'Ya should be more careful and not be drinking so fast.' I was clutching my stomach. It was on fire.

'It's not lemonade,' I croaked.

'Watcha mean?' says Aunt Lil.

'It's not lemonade,' I repeated. Aunt Lil smelt the bottle and took a little swig. 'Oh Holy Dublin,' she proclaimed, 'it's poteen.'

'Quick,' she ordered, 'get sick as quick as ya can. Go out there in the yard and put your fingers down yer neck.'

By now I was feeling a warm glow and the pain had gone. 'Ah, I'm alright,' says I. 'I won't die this time.'

'Go on and do as I tell ya now,' Aunt Lil pressed. 'If your mother learns about this. Oh, Cross o' God.' Aunt Lil blessed herself twice. Then I began to recite the Proclamation of Independence of the Irish Republic in Gaelic, mimicking the heroes of the 1916 rebellion. 'Oh Holy Dublin,' Aunt Lil proclaimed desperately, 'I'll be shot when your mother finds out. And what'll your father say and him not a drinker.'

I winked at her and put my index finger to my mouth to signify solidarity. I was beyond caring that she couldn't see. 'When boyhood fire was in my blood,' I began singing and then forgot the words. Then the room began spinning. I tried to focus on the open fire but it kept moving from right to left. The last thing I remember was trying not to close my eyes but deciding I should anyway.

I woke up the next day at home in my bed, not knowing how I got there. When I tried to move I couldn't. The pain was too great. Finally my mother came into the room. 'Fancy that one giving a young lad like you a cup of poteen. It could have killed you.'

'Water,' I croaked.

'Ya can't have water,' my mother told me. 'I spoke to Kieran before I left and he said the only thing I could give you was a bottle of Guinness. God knows but he's had enough experience with cures like that.' Ma opened a bottle of Guinness and poured it into a glass. It was all head but I didn't care. I just needed liquid. I sucked through the froth and found the cool, bitter liquid beneath it. It tasted like nectar. 'Not so quick,' says Ma, 'or you'll only be getting sick again.' By the time I had finished the bottle, the warm glow was back and I could have kicked football for Ireland. And so it was, at the age of fifteen I sang my first rebel song whilst drunk.

The slide to adolescence was almost imperceptible. One day I was excited by everything my life and the town of Birr had to offer. The next day I was looking in McNamara's shop window, just down the road from ours, and I saw my reflection. I hated it. 'Ma?' says I. 'Am I good-looking?'

'Would ya be off out of that,' says she. 'Most people are happy to have their health.' That was all I needed. My ugliness was confirmed. While most of the lads were talking about kissing girls and playing spin the bottle, all I wanted to do was to die because I had just grown another spot—right where it could be noticed.

I began to hate appearing on stage even though the crowds always seemed to shout for an encore. And to top it all I was no good at games. Whenever a team was being picked in school for either hurling or football, I was the last person to be picked.

I decided to do something about it. 'Ma,' says I, clutching my GI Joe comic book, 'there's an advertisement here for Charles Atlas. Ya know, he gives you things to build up your body.'

'A bleddy muscle man, ya want to be now. Sure wouldn't that be the greatest waste of money ever?' Sam overheard the conversation and started calling me geranium.

'Feck off stumpy,' says I. But everyone knew that Sam was really good-looking so the insult had no effect. I began to find escape in films and just loved courtroom dramas. Perry Mason wasn't the best-looking man on Earth but everyone liked him because he was really smart. I decided that I would become a barrister and be really incisive like Perry. In any event, I concluded, the wig would hide my embarrassment.

Because I had to perform on stage I was not allowed to grow my hair long until I was seventeen. It was then that I met Anne. Anne Finlay was the most gorgeous creature I had ever known and was the first girl I ever loved. I can remember asking her to dance. It was at a marquee dance in the little village of Cloghan. All the girls were lined up one side of the hall and all the fellas bunched together on the other side.

Big Tom and the Mainliners struck up 'The Fields of Athenry' and the stampede began. Buffeted as if in a swell, I was catapulted towards this girl that was standing with a group of girls. 'Would ya like to dance?' says I expecting a refusal.

'Love to,' says she.

She was so easy to talk to. She loved the things I did— reading modern English novels. She even liked Alastair Maclean. I had never met a girl before who had even known his name let alone worshipped his genius as I did. She also liked the Bronte sisters; she had even struggled with Proust —just like me.

We left the dance floor and went outside for some air. She was so perfect. Long flowing hair, dancing brown eyes and a laugh that made me weak. We talked for hours but it seemed like minutes, and when it was time to go home we vowed to meet again. Then she kissed me.

I am sure it is not the reaction she expected but I became so overwhelmed with emotion that a tear flowed down my right cheek. 'You okay?' she asked.

'More than okay,' says I. I was. I was happy that this gorgeous creature did not see me as the ugly duckling I thought I was.

Anne and I dated over two years until she went to England to train as a teacher. Our love did not survive the distance but to this day I think of her, where she might be and what she might be doing. But I will always thank her for releasing me from the bondage of my self-imagined ugliness.

Chapter Two

When I was growing up there were two types of Irish people —Culshees, who were people that came from outside the Pale, and Jackeens, who had funny accents, thought milk came from bottles and lived in Dublin. 'How come Culsher's have red necks?' my cousin who came from Dublin once asked.

'Don't know,' says I.

'Because their mammies beat them across the back of the neck and shouts, "Get up to Dublin and get a job." '

Culshees invariably worked in the Civil Defence Service whereas Jackeens normally went to either Liverpool or London. I was determined not to become a civil servant, so I joined the firm of Calor-Kosangas as an assistant accountant. Calor-Kosangas was Ireland's largest supplier of liquid petroleum gas to both the domestic and commercial sectors.

I was there only a few days when the chief accountant, Bob Hayes, called me to his office. 'So, you want to be an accountant?' Bob asked. I nodded but my answer wasn't strictly true.

The world of business seemed like a giant puzzle to me and I wanted to learn everything there was to know about it. I was convinced that only knowledge could yield the solution.

'Accountancy is about credibility,' he told me. 'Accountants must be analytical and reflective. They must constantly
search for facts that will inform a better way forward for the
business. I agreed with him. 'So what you have to do is to
take all that theory you learned at college and give it a prac-
tical focus, and the only focus you need is fact.'

I wasn't so sure about that. My days in our shop in Birr had
taught me that the greatest asset a businessman could have
was the ability to listen. But Bob was a pure accountant, and
unlike me, had no aspirations to explore the wider aspects
of business.

Bob was a smallish man with greying hair and he constantly pushed his grey-rimmed spectacles back on the
bridge of his nose. 'Any questions?' he asked.

'Not at the moment,' I replied. 'But this is my first job and
I'm anxious to learn.'

'Good. Then you can help me with this project I am working on.' I felt relieved that I had at least said the right things
and I assured him I would welcome any opportunity to
learn. 'I want to look at transport costs,' he told me. 'I think
there may be an opportunity for some savings. Interested in
helping?'

That night I told the chaps with whom I was sharing an
apartment about this great project for which I had been
specially chosen. 'It could save the company hundreds of
thousands of pounds,' I boasted. One of them worked at the
Office of the Collector General and he was drooling at the
thought of increased tax yield. The other, who was completing his articles at a leading firm of chartered accountants, gave me advice on how to keep the windfall safe from
the sticky clutches of our flatmate.

I felt alive, a part of something vibrant and meaningful,

and my veins throbbed with a desire to succeed. The next day I reported to Bob's office. 'How can I help?' I asked.

'First thing is go home and put on an old shirt and jeans. When you come back I want you to go down to the archives and dig out all the transport invoices for the past six years. I want you to prepare a report on the cost of each truck and the number of cylinders of gas each carried.'

I spent the next six weeks inhaling dust mites and sneezing. But I completed my report. I got one of the secretaries to type it up for me and I presented it to Bob. 'Looks all right to me,' he said. 'Good job. I'll let you have a copy of my report when it's finished.' A week later I got a copy of Bob's report with a covering memo thanking me for my input. I thumbed through it and found what I was looking for. My contribution took up two lines of the finished article, but to me they were the most important two lines ever written.

I showed the report to my flatmates that evening. 'It didn't save hundreds of thousands,' the taxman complained. 'In fact, it seems to confirm that the current method of operation is the most efficient.' I didn't care. My two lines were still the most important!

After Birr, the nightlife in Dublin was very exciting. Many is the night I spent at the Wexford Inn on Dame Street or the Crossguns Pub in Phibsborough, listening to Horslips or the Dubliners as they traced the history of my great nation through its trials and tribulations. Sometimes I would hear notes just like my father used to play for me and I would get up and dance. I felt a part of something that was growing, and Ireland was growing faster than it had ever done before.

Although Bob Hayes was a man who was small in stature, he was big in intellect. 'When you come to the point where you feel you can no longer learn any more,' he once told me, 'then you must leave immediately.'

'Why is that?' I asked.

'Because when you feel you can learn nothing more, you no longer possess the qualities you need to help others learn. Once you have reached this point, the organisation doesn't benefit from your best efforts. Therefore,' he concluded, 'you are better off somewhere else.'

'But I'm still learning,' I assured him.

'Indeed you are, young man. And if you're lucky, you will hold that curiosity for the rest of your life.' I smiled but Bob remained solemn.

'You have a great gift, Tom. You need to find a place that knows no limits; that can stretch you to near breaking point and then some. A mind like yours, left to its own devices, will destroy you.'

'How do you know?' I asked.

'I have seen many a young lad go through my department over the years. They all wanted to head for greater things. Some of them did and some didn't. But you can be anything you want to be ... so long as it doesn't bore you.' I laughed. 'One day I hope you find something that keeps your interest.'

'Ya,' says I, 'making pots of money.'

'No, I don't think so. Money will never be enough for you.'

Dublin
Autumn 1976

I had been dating my college sweetheart for nearly three years. She, like me, came from the Midlands and we did everything together—going out with friends, dancing the night away at the Zhivago Club on Lower Bagott Street. Cora looked absolutely stunning in her tight, flared jeans and platform shoes. I thought I was the bee's knees in my patterned pink ties.

We shared nearly everything; our hopes and dreams. What I didn't share was my view of life. Cora saw life as a balanced journey where responsibilities were taken seriously and discharged. I continued to see life as an adventure to be experienced. But I was willing to change just to be with her and we married in the cathedral in Mullingar on the last day of October 1976.

Our first son, Stephen, was born two and a half years later and I was more convinced than ever that my adventure-seeking was just a passing phase. He was the most wonderful, most vulnerable bundle of goodness that God could grant anyone. We were so, so proud.

I remember the first time the nurse at the Portiuncla Hospital in Ballinasloe handed him to me. 'It's your son, Mister Pey,' says she.

I was choked. 'Hey, little fella,' says I. 'I'll be the best daddy in the world.' I think he believed me.

Portarlington
April 1979

I arrived at Avon's Irish subsidiary via a number of middle-management positions in the motor and pharmaceutical industries. 'We're very pleased to have you here,' Mike Talaska, an athletic American with black, sculpted hair, told me on my first day at the Portarlington plant. 'We can sure use experience like yours.'

Within a year I was promoted to financial director and within another year I took on responsibility for production support activities. At last I had an opportunity to use all of my acquired skills and some more. Avon encouraged innovation and I took to it like a duck to water. I learned all about quality systems, industrial engineering techniques and in return I helped them control costs to the point where the Irish plant was to become one of the most efficient in the Avon world.

Then one day the vice president in charge of our division came to my office. He was a slim, neat man with deep religious convictions, which he often expressed in his long Wisconsin accent. 'I think Head Office should meet you,' he told me. 'I'd like a couple of the senior guys to get an opportunity to have a chat with you and work out a career plan for you. How would you feel about that?'

I was earning over forty thousand a year, had a 3.5 litre Toyota Crown, a non-contributory pension scheme and an expense account that was more than generous. I didn't think it got much better than that. 'Great,' I replied. I tried not to sound too excited.

Forty-second Street was everything the song promised. Glitz and escapism at the Times Square end, a testament to how low humanity can sink at the other. 'New York, they tell me,' Aunt Lil once said, 'is a place of hope and hopelessness.' Forty-second Street was all of that on one boulevard.

But there was something electric about the city. Having left the fresh air at Shannon Airport less than ten hours previously I was seduced by a horn-honking, siren-filled hedonism. I knew I had arrived at a place where my soul could express itself and that longing for adventure I had done my best to suppress returned with the ache of an unsatisfied addiction.

For the first night I walked the streets, ignoring the instructions of Head Office staff not to wander into situations I didn't understand. 'And remember,' they told me, 'eye contact is dangerous.' This I found difficult to understand. Where I came from you looked everyone in the eye and bid them a fine day. Not to do so was discourteous. It seemed that they not only drove on the wrong side of the road in this city, but friendliness was seen as a sign of aggression or, even worse, weakness. Yet I felt excited by the latent danger.

My neck creaked at the height of the buildings, and any thoughts of home and Ireland were replaced with an obsession to be part of the electricity that was Manhattan.

It was about two o'clock in the morning when I returned to my hotel on Central Park South. My head was filled with the essence of the city, and the rude behaviour of its people. My room was on the fifteenth floor. I had never slept that high before and felt a little uncomfortable lest the building would collapse. But a plaque in the foyer boasted that the hotel had been standing for more than fifty years. I relaxed and entered the elevator. The lobby was still alive with people and lazy piano music drifted from the bar, but the long journey was taking its toll. I made my way to the lift and to bed. As the elevator doors were about to close, a very attractive lady squeezed her way through. She turned and smiled at me.

'Jesus,' I swore inwardly, 'it's Linda Gray.' I was struck dumb. I wanted to say, 'How do you do, Linda? I think you're great.' But I couldn't open my mouth. I revisit that moment many times and still curse my shyness. But this was New York —so what the heck!

Next morning I jumped out of bed and into the shower. I turned on the steaming liquid and was nearly knocked off my feet by its force. Back home the showers dribbled on you! When I adjusted to the shower pressure I began coughing. Then I saw the sign telling users to keep the bathroom door opened when taking a shower to allow the chlorine in the water to escape. At home our water came from a spring well that was sunk to the side of our house and was as clear as crystal.

I left the hotel at eight fifteen the next morning horrified at the price they were asking for breakfast—twenty dollars! 'If you walk around Fifty-second Street,' the doorman told me, 'you will find a place that'll give you a good breakfast for a quarter of the price.' His name was Donal and he had come from Tipperary about ten years ago.

The Manhattan atmosphere was even more electric than I had remembered it from the previous evening. The air felt warm and smelt of sulphur, and cars changed lanes as irritated motorists honked horns. The cacophony of traffic sounds and sirens was a perfect accompaniment to the hordes of people who filed to work. They were made up of all colours, races and sizes and it was nothing like I had even experienced in Dublin. They all looked and acted as if the rest of life and humanity was none of their business.

An attractive lady dressed in tight dark sports gear dodged through the inching traffic on roller skates. I walked along Fifty-second Street and spotted the Seventh Avenue Eatery. It looked clean and welcoming and the notice in the window offered all-day breakfast for six dollars. I could identify with that sort of price.

As the glass entrance doors closed behind me, it felt as if I had entered a new world—one that was quieter and cooler. 'What can I get you, Mac?' His accent was nasal and he looked like Kojak without the lollipop.

'Two eggs, a couple of rashers, black pudding and toast,' says I, rubbing my hands in anticipation.

'You speak friggin' English or what?' he snapped.

'Huh?'

'You want black pudding you go somewhere else. Okay?'

'Em ...'

'How you want your eggs?'

'Soft,' says I.

'Jesus H ... Sunny or over easy?'

'Whatever.' I wanted the ground to swallow me.

'Look, guy. It's simple. You only have two choices.' I looked bewildered. 'Tell ya what I do. Why don't I make two nice big eyes with sunny eggs, arrange the sausage like a big friggin' smiley mouth and the bacon like hair. Okay?'

'You don't need to go to so much trouble,' says I. He swore again and looked down the length of the counter along the line of mostly empty, blue resin-covered stools. The few customers paid no attention.

'You believe this guy?' he shouted. 'Wants a friggin' work of art. Hey, buddie, you want to eat or not?' He roared with laughter. I perspired with embarrassment.

'Look, you shit,' I spat 'You serve breakfast or just crap?'

'The man's got a voice,' he declared. 'Welcome to New York, Paddy. Have a nice day.' He didn't charge me for breakfast and every time I visited New York after that I ate at the Seventh Avenue Eatery. Joe retired about five years ago and I miss his unique New York charm. We still exchange Christmas cards.

That evening, after a boring day in the Purchasing Department learning how important everyone's job was, I took a cab to Wall Street. It was seven o'clock and the wine bars were filled with excited chatter. The Street seemed narrower and more claustrophobic than uptown Manhattan but I felt drawn to the place. It almost felt more at home to me than Portarlington. I loved the feeling of risk and excitement that seemed to ooze from the walls of the tall buildings.

I went into one of the bars, found a seat at the counter and ordered a Perrier 'on the rocks'. 'How long have you been on the wagon?' the barman asked. I smiled but didn't answer.

An attractive, dark-haired girl sat in the seat beside me ordered a tequila slammer. I smiled at her and then began looking around the bar at the young pinstriped graduates who were engaged in deep and heated conversation. 'You friggin' queer or what?' the lady shouted at me.

'Huh?'

She gulped her drink and left the bar angry and mortally wounded.

'Married, eh?' The voice was soft and Scottish.

'Andrew Patmore's the name and I hail from sunny Edinburgh.' He extended his hand and I shook it. 'Married?' he repeated.

'Yes. One son.'

'It showed.'

'What do you mean?'

'That girl fancied you. That's why she got angry when you didn't buy her the drink.'

'Funny custom,' says I.

'Don't worry, lad. It gets stranger.' I introduced myself to Andrew. 'You working the Street?' he asked.

'No. Senior manager with Avon.'

'Pack it in, lad. Look round you here. These kids earn more than the chief executive of Avon. Poor bastards burn out in a couple of years but they're rich.'

'How do they get jobs like that?' I asked.

'They're Ivy Leagues. America's first brains.'

'Feels more like a meat market,' I concluded.

'Aye, laddie, it is that. The world's most expensive butcher's shop.'

That evening I ate dinner with Andrew at the Windows of the World on top of the World Trade Center. He was doing a doctorate at Edinburgh and was studying the emerging junk bond markets. 'You ever met Milken?' I asked.

'Once. The man's a genius. One feels alive just being in his presence.'

'Where did he get the idea?' I asked.

'Hell only knows. It makes a mockery of rational economics. But then people are always prepared to gamble. But the crazy thing is, he's getting the big banks interested as well. I just hope it doesn't all end in tears.'

We spent the rest of the evening discussing the finer points of balance sheet leverage over dinner. By the end of the evening the broad-faced, six-foot, wavy-haired Scot and I became good friends. I knew I had to be involved with the excitement that was the world of finance.

Galway
Summer 1986

The city of Galway is one of the most beautiful places on Earth. Each morning as I drove to work at the local crystal company I saw the orange reflection of the rising sun on the blue waters of the Gulf Stream. Each evening, as I returned, I watched the sun go down on Galway Bay.

By this time my second son was born. We called him Adrian after a famous Irish television producer, Adrian Cronin. He produced a number of shows on Irish television that featured Dad and me in those days when we performed together. They seemed like a long time ago and even longer because I knew that the closest landmass west of Galway was America and I knew that an important part of me was there. I began to get feelings of claustrophobia and I began to imagine that the horizon was so close to me I would suffocate.

But then I would get home and just being with my boys seemed to give me a renewed sense of purpose and I buried my dreams in the realities of day-to-day living.

I rang Andrew one evening. He now held a senior position with Goldman Sachs in New York and I loved to chat with him and wallow in his gossip like a frustrated voyager. I often did this. We spoke for a long time about the rises and falls of the world stock markets, and the witch hunts for insider traders. 'It's not like the markets move on much else other than inside information. Anyway, we all have to be whiter than white now.'

'What makes professionals like you invest in a project?' I asked him.

'The certainty of making money,' he retorted. We laughed. 'Do you have something in mind?' he asked.

72

'No,' I replied, a little too quickly.

'You sure?'

'I don't,' I replied, honestly. 'But would you invest in a person like me?'

Pause.

'Maybe. Maybe not. To be honest,' he told me, 'I wouldn't get involved with you simply because I know you. But if you had a good proposition I would advise you where to go with it.'

About a month later I was talking to one of my old colleagues from the Irish subsidiary of Avon. He was a Canadian and had returned to the States and had been offered a severance package. 'Gone past my sell-by date,' he laughed.

'So what are you going to do?' I enquired.

'Go back to Canada, buy a store and hibernate.'

Then we came up with the idea of buying the subsidiary. I don't know whose idea it was. It just seemed to form as we tossed ideas around. 'I'll put out a few feelers,' my Canadian friend promised, 'and I'll get back to you.'

I spent the next week writing down everything I knew about the company, trying desperately to make it look like an investment prospect. But whatever way I figured it the answer came out the same. Avon would never sell at a loss but the full book value was just too expensive to make it viable.

It was a Sunday evening, the family had just finished dinner and we were preparing to settle down to watch 'Glenroe' on television. The phone rang. It was my Canadian friend. 'I spoke with one of the executive VPs in New York. Guess what? He liked the idea.'

'And you?'

'Too rich for my blood. Besides that store and hibernation beckons. But good luck anyway.'

I rang Andrew and got his answering machine. I asked him to call back as soon as he could. A week later he returned my call. 'Sorry, laddie, but I've been in the Bahamas.'

'Business or pleasure?' says I.

'Business is always pleasure in the Bahamas.'

I told him about my idea. 'Slow down,' he told me. 'This could be good or this could be bad.'

'How do you mean?' I asked.

'We'll need to structure the deal on paper, see if it works. Then we'll have to run it past a few people and see if there is any interest. Then we need to talk to the corporation.'

'Sounds fine to me,' I said enthusiastically.

'When can you be in New York?' The question knocked the wind from my sails. It was a reasonable request but the implication was dropping everything, including family, and doing business. The reality of this was just beginning to sink in. I felt an unusual mixture of guilt and elation—both at the same time.

'Well I . . .'

'Look Tom. If you want to be a businessman you need to take a risk. Sometimes it pays off. Most times it doesn't. You've got to choose.'

The little voice in my head that had always stood me in good stead was silent. 'Soon as I can get a flight. This week sometime.'

'You can stay with me, laddie. Welcome to the world of the big boys.'

I'm not really sure how my family felt about the prospect of me just taking off to New York. In truth, I don't believe either Cora or myself really considered the probability of me succeeding in acquiring the Avon factory or the fact that I would probably become self-employed. If we had, I think I would not have bought the ticket.

But the blood was soaring in my veins and I was beginning to feel really alive inside. It made me realize how dead I had been up to then, and I now realize that this was the point where I had made an unconscious decision to follow my dreams. Once I had decided upon this there was no going back.

New York was as exhilarating as ever. Andrew had sent a car to the airport for me and as it drove over Brooklyn Bridge I felt as if I could own the world. That evening we grabbed a show on Broadway and Andrew refused to discuss business until after we had eaten dinner. 'Did you see that magician?' he asked me. I nodded, my mouth full of pasta. 'That's what real finance is about. The quickness of the hand and all that.'

'What ever do you mean, Andrew?' I asked.

Andrew had drunk a couple of glasses of wine and was in full flow. 'There are many ways of constructing a balance sheet. It's like an artist who has a blank canvas. His genius is in the way he mixes his colours and applies the paint to the canvas.'

'But surely a balance sheet is a balance sheet,' I protested.

'Surely nothing, laddie. The world of American finance is the world of the possible. Never forget that.' I raised my eyebrows. Watching Andrew work was like watching a master architect construct a model of his creation. He worked with the information I provided and asked me many more questions. He always asked why, whenever I made a statement. 'It's easy figuring out how,' he told me. 'Why is where the real money is made.'

He worked days and came back to his apartment in the

evening, showered and changed into casual clothes, ate dinner and then began working on the project with me. One evening, when I was about to give up and go home because of a yawning lack of any real progress, he told me he thought it might just work. 'I've got to go home,' I told him. 'My family is expecting me and I miss the kids.'

Andrew's face stiffened. 'If this is not the single most important thing in your life then it won't work.'

'I'll be back in a week,' I promised.

Back in Galway the pace seemed slower and the horizons seemed closer than ever. My wife thought the whole idea was crazy, but I was gripped by a determination that bordered on obsessive. 'Don't you see,' I reasoned with her. 'This is my big chance—our big chance.' That night she cried herself to sleep and the guilt wrenched my guts until I could feel nothing, only a burning excitement.

I finished what I had to do at my employers' and took two weeks' holiday. They didn't mind. The place was running well and I was on the verge of delivering a prize for them that once they only dreamed of. 'What's the attraction in America?' the chairman asked me. He was a highly respected retired politician.

'Just chasing a bit of business,' I told him. 'Private stuff.'

He nodded wisely. 'You have a great talent, Tom. You have a talent that can make a reality of the dreams of others. Take my advice and don't waste it chasing your own.' I felt a dagger in my stomach and I couldn't pull it out. I was filled with self-doubt and cancelled my flight to New York. Andrew was as mad as hell.

I threw myself into my work and in three months I had

completed the transformation of the company from an over-traded skeleton to one with a vibrant future. But as the workload subsided, the gnawing in my soul began to ache and I could think of nothing, only getting back to New York.

I rang an old finance professor of mine and asked his advice. 'You really want this company?' he asked.

'Of course. Why do you ask?'

'Because sometimes we like the chase and the reality becomes a disappointment. Remember, when you take on a company you become responsible for the lives of others. Don't mess around with the lives of innocent people who don't have the resources to protect themselves.'

'I wouldn't do that,' I promised.

'You mightn't, but if you get into a pool with sharks then someone is bound to get hurt.'

'Andrew Patmore is a friend,' I insisted.

'Mister Patmore is a professional,' he replied.

A week later I was back in New York and could think of nothing else but taking over the company in Ireland. 'What are you going to do with it when you get it?' Andrew asked me one evening.

'Make money. I don't know, work it efficiently.'

'Balderdash,' he scorned. 'Sell it on. Let someone else do the drudge. Keep a small interest in it if you like. But turn it over. I could possibly find someone to buy it from you.' Professor Corrigan's advice rang loudly in my ears. Friendship played no part in business. Not in Wall Street at any rate.

Avon agreed to meet and I offered them full book value on the basis that they took a note on the company that was repayable over five years. The only catch was that they had to provide sufficient business to ensure that there was enough cash to meet the obligations of the debt.

They didn't flinch and said they would consider it. One of their tax experts told me that he couldn't support the deal because the tax implications were too great. Ireland was a tax haven for manufacturing companies that exported their goods. The trouble was that both Andrew and I recognized this benefit as well. But it was clear that we were in for a long and exhaustive round of negotiations. That didn't bother us. The fact was, we needed the time to get our backers in place.

The only problem was that I continued to talk of Andrew and me as a team whereas he introduced himself as an individual who represented me. Given Corrigan's words I decided that when the time was right, Andrew would have to decide whether he was a professional or a team player. It was clear, however, that business at this level had no room for anyone who tried to be both. 'Can't solve your tax problems,' I told him as we parted at the entrance to Nine, West Fifty-seventh Street.

Trying to buy a business was an expensive racket and soon I began to eat into the money we had saved for our kids' future. I knew this couldn't continue and my wife was getting more and more agitated but said less and less. But I was a man driven by something deep inside me that devoured my soul. I focused on nothing but business and flying to New York and Boston as and when Andrew needed me or the business dictated.

Even when I played with my sons I ate, drank and drowned in thoughts of acquiring the Avon plant. 'Why do you want the damned thing?' Ma asked me one day.

'I don't know, Ma,' says I. 'I suppose I want it because it's there.'

'That doesn't make anything worthwhile, son,' says she. 'All that does is feed your ambition to win. And winnin' is no good to ya unless the prize does somethin' for ya.'

'Like what?' says I.

'Like makin' ya a better person and not just a richer one.'

'I can make this place work, Ma,' says I. 'I know I can.'

'So what's the challenge, then?'

I couldn't answer her. I knew I couldn't put all my eggs in the one basket and my available cash was running out, so I started up a small business selling bankrupt stock.

This got a grand reasonably quickly and soon I had a regular income that I used to cover the acquisition expenses that were mounting. Andrew had introduced me to a number of private investors in Boston and they seemed keen but demanded money updates and even more reviews to business plans. Still the deal I struck with them was satisfactory and they were fully committed to it.

'Are you in or out?' I asked Andrew one evening. He had flown up to Boston and we both had driven down to Newport, Rhode Island, for the weekend. It was late summer and we ate a fresh fish supper under canvas at the home of one of the investors. His house was bigger that most European mansions and when he said we would eat by the pool, he forgot to mention this was a mini lake. The three-storeyed twenty-bedroomed home stood in thirty perfectly manicured acres.

Jim Winberg was small, extremely energetic and as hard as nails. 'I was a millionaire by the time I was eighteen,' he told me. 'By the time I was thirty I owned eleven companies with a total turnover of over two hundred and fifty million dollars. Today I invest.' My admiration was obvious. 'I like you,' he told me. 'You and I could do some serious business together.'

And that was when I began to separate the reality from the dream of life in the commercial fast lane. The fact was that Jim lived alone. His previous two marriages had split up and he had no children. I wanted it all, a family and the business, and I was determined to have both.

The negotiations with Avon took nearly six months. I had resigned my job in Ireland and had spent nearly all of our money financing the expenses of the takeover. I pushed Avon for a decision and they declined our offer. The taxman had won.

'You can never know what it's like to succeed,' Andrew told me as I prepared to board a plane from Kennedy, 'until you have tasted failure.' I shook his hand in silence. Now I knew what the Old Professor meant when he said Andrew Patmore was a professional. I had gambled everything we had on a dream and I had lost. The losses sustained in the failed Avon takeover and on another investment I had made in the jewellery industry meant I was broke and I needed to start again.

Chapter Three

London

February 1990

Shaken but unstirred I sat down and analysed what had gone wrong and, more importantly, what I could learn from the experience. The answers came and I didn't like what was emerging.

Firstly, it was clear that I went in over my head. I failed to apply the complexities of financial engineering and it was clear that if I wished to succeed in the world of takeovers and mergers, I would need to demonstrate considerable expertise in this area.

Secondly, I had failed to grasp the point that multinationals liked to protect their money from greedy governments for as long as possible. I understood international tax law but again bowed to professionals like Andrew who should merely have been allowed to act as advisor and middleman.

Thirdly, I had negotiated as if I were still an employee. I needed to adopt a more professional approach.

The list went on and on and depressed me. However, I knew I yearned for the world of deals, for a world where enterprises could be built from dreams. I would require the expertise to participate, so there was no option but to go back to school.

With the little money left to me I stepped up activity in the small company that traded in bankrupt and salvaged stock. I stuck to the old adage—when in doubt revert to what you know! I knew retailing. I was born into the trade.

The company wasn't a huge success but it made enough to keep the wolf from the door and I used my spare time to brush up on international taxation and the rules of international investment banking. I had opened the door to a world that was both limitless and exhilarating, and now there was no going back.

The activities of the company meant that I travelled a lot throughout the UK and Central Europe. Most of the people I came into contact with had no time for loftier pursuits. They simply wanted to buy something for a pound and sell it for two. But every now and again I met senior bankers and this is how I met Peter Van Dam, an investment banker with Credit Lyonnais in Amsterdam. 'If you are serious about going into this game,' he told me, 'forget New York and get yourself into London. With your knowledge and experience you should have no problem getting a good start.'

By this time my marriage had broken up and there was nothing to tie me to Ireland any longer except my children. But the shame of failure weighed heavily upon me. I equated successful fatherhood with commercial good fortune and against that yardstick I was an all-round failure. I needed to prove to them that their Dad could be a good father.

Peter agreed to introduce me to 'some people' he knew in London and through them I met Peter Avery, an ex senior banker at Lloyd's and a founder member of a very large bank in the Gulf. Peter was heading up a small but exclusive private partnership that offered financial planning and merchant banking advice to a select client group. 'We'll try you out,' Peter agreed after a very pleasant lunch at the Dorchester. 'If it goes well, we can talk about a more permanent arrangement. Say in six months?' I shook his hand warmly and gratefully.

My first client was an Austrian businessman who wanted to conduct business in Moscow. I learned very quickly about the darker side of commerce but steered the client through a successful venture. He asked that I be permanently assigned to his work with us. In addition to paying Peter's huge fee he gave me two and a half percent of the profits—for luck!

That night I decided that my tiny, badly heated studio flat in Forest Hill, South-east London, was too small and I found a two-bedroomed maisonette in a nice neighbourhood in Lewisham. Now I could invite my boys over to stay. Even though I spoke to them on the telephone every week, I missed them like hell.

My second client wanted to buy a small radio station in Texas. I travelled out to Houston, took a look around and examined the books. In a word, it sucked! 'I will advise my client to pay no more than a hundred thousand dollars,' I told the proprietors.

'We could get ten times that from some of the big boys,' they replied. They knew this wasn't true and they knew that I knew.

'That's my final offer. My client would, however, be prepared to make a rather substantial investment in the station and get it back on its feet. I'm sure he would require good management.' And that was that. They were interested but wanted to know the details, especially the details of their management contracts.

When I got back to London I reported to Peter. He approved of my approach and told me to talk to the client. 'I haven't got that type of money,' the client complained when we added the cost of acquisition to the cost of rebuilding the station. He needed over two million dollars.

'No,' I agreed, 'but I know a man that has.'

And Andrew Patmore obliged with mezzanine funding as I reorganized the balance sheet and sold on the radio station on behalf of my client, who retained a twenty percent stake. Our partnership got a five percent stake in the relaunched station and this was easily worth a quarter of a million dollars. Everyone was happy and I was made a partner in the firm. I was on the way back.

I was only two months in my comfortable maisonette when it became too small. I had met a wonderful woman who is my partner today and we decided to set up house in Bromley. At least I could live in a house and invite my children over to visit their Dad and be proud of him. All I had to do was to continue to recognize that I was good at helping other people realize their dreams, and any ambitions of personal ownership would need to be put on hold for a moment. Anyway, I was now a full partner with Peter in a partnership that was growing in both stature and value. My children came to visit me and we spent three wonderful weeks together. When it came time for them to go home, my heart broke in three places and it hurt.

A businessman is only ever as good as his secretary. A good secretary organizes your day so effectively that you both almost become one person. So when Peter and I agreed that I should hire a PA, I took great care over the appointment.

Julie was elegant, extremely well spoken and extremely efficient in a caring way. I loved her sense of humour and very soon my clients began to value her as much as I did.

It was a warm July day and the sunlight streamed through my office window, tempting me to sit by the Serpentine and let the world drift by. 'A Professor Greenberg to see you,' Julie said. 'He doesn't have an appointment but says he is a friend of Countess von Hatzenberg'

'Oh well,' I sighed, 'I suppose I could see him.'

'I'll ask him to wait ten minutes.'

The Countess was an ageing yet formidable woman who was obviously used to getting her own way. I had met her at a diplomatic dinner I attended in Geneva. 'My husband made more money than I could spend,' she told me. 'Now I invest some of it in the furtherance of humanity.' I nodded my approval. 'Perhaps your firm can help,' she said in a way that suggested the idea had not just entered her head. A diplomatic gathering is not a place where spontaneity just simply occurs.

I explained to her that our partnership was rather small and didn't have the type of money that could yet make a difference. 'It's your expertise, young man,' she told me. 'I want your brain and not your money.'

'Any time,' I told her. The Countess could, if nurtured, be a good source of clients.

Professor Alexander Greenberg was a small, dapper man who had greyed with dignity. He sported a moustache which complemented his darting blue eyes and left one in no doubt that the man was caring, intelligent and fun to be with. 'Professor Greenberg,' I said, my hand outstretched.

'Alex,' he replied quietly but confidently. 'You can call me Alex.'

I felt totally disarmed. 'How can I help, Alex?' I asked.

'I would love a cup of tea,' he replied. His eyes twinkled mischievously.

'I'd kill for one myself, Alex,' says I.

As we tucked into tea and biscuits, Alexander Greenberg OBE told me a lot about himself. He was married for over forty years; his children, now grown up, lived in Israel. He was a paediatrician, practised in Harley Street for many years, was vice president of an organization that represented his profession on a worldwide basis, and helped found a clinic in North London to help children with cerebral palsy live as independently and as fully as possible and to train their carers to assist in this project.

'A couple of year ago,' he began, 'I raised some money with a group of people to build a hospital in Tel Aviv. We acquired a site close to the Israeli parliament and we have constructed a building on it. But we have run out of money.'

'I see. So you need to raise sufficient capital to complete the building and acquire the necessary equipment and staff?' I concluded.

'Yes,' he replied enthusiastically.

'I have never financed a hospital before,' I told him, ' and I have no idea of Israeli law in relation to lending and taking security. But since the Countess has introduced you, perhaps I can ask around. Have you tried any of the Israeli banks?'

Greenberg's mischievous eyes flashed with anger. 'We are not looking for a loan. Children need care at an affordable price not at private medicine rates.'

'I see,' I replied tactfully. 'How can we help then?'

'I need to raise thirty-five million pounds and the Countess believes this can be done by trading bank paper. She said that you could assist in this matter.'

'Bank paper?' I asked.

'Prime banknotes and stand-by letters of credit,' he replied as if I knew everything about trading these securities.

'I'm sorry,' I replied. 'I'm aware of these instruments of course. However, I do not understand how the Countess means to trade them. I am assuming she has title to such instruments and wishes to use them as security?'

Professor Greenberg was beginning to think he had made a mistake. 'I believe it was a bit more involved than that,' he replied. There was no acidity in his tone, just disinterest.

'Why don't I talk to the Countess, see what she has in mind and get back to you? Let's say in a week's time.' Alex smiled again. This time it was out of courtesy. He shook my hand and left.

The meeting had taken half an hour, so I felt I had earned the perfect excuse to bunk off and spend the remainder of the day sitting in the tea room at the Serpentine, thinking of Greenberg and his simplistic model of wealth creation.

The next morning I arrived at the office late. 'You look tired,' Julie said.

'So what?' I snapped.

'Nothing. Just worried. That's all.'

'Sorry,' I relented. 'It's just that Greenberg. He's really gotten inside of my head.'

'Why?' she asked.

'Oh, never mind. It's too complicated. Can you get Countess von Hatzenberg on the phone.'

'Is she in London?'

'I don't know,' I replied. 'But try her home in Austria and if not try the usual London hotel. If she is not in either, she may even be in Venezuela.'

Ten minutes later Julie interrupted my morning cup of coffee. 'Sorry, Tom, I can't track her down, but I'll keep trying. Your ten thirty will be here in ten minutes. Do you want me to hold him?'

'No. I'll be fine, thank you. Just feeling a little tired, that's all. I think I'll take a couple of days and go to Ireland. You know, visit the kids'

'I think it would be a good idea,' she told me. 'You've hardly had a day off in the past three months. Mimi will appreciate time with you.'

I was feeling bunged up with a fluey feeling and my place on the ladder of success had made me selfish. I had totally ignored how my partner would be feeling about the amount of time I had been spending at work. A few days in Ireland would do us both good. Although Mimi was Goan by birth, her mum lived in Ireland. She could visit her mum and I could visit my boys and the rest of my family.

Julie said that she would book the tickets for that weekend. 'Heathrow okay?' She didn't wait for a reply.

The plane trip to Ireland was uncomfortable. My flu had gotten worse and I felt as if my sinuses would explode. I began seeing grey spots in my eyes. Mimi, who is a nurse, told me I should see a doctor as soon as I arrived and get something that would relieve the symptoms. I took two aspirin and that appeared to help.

The weekend went well. My boys were happy to see me and I them. We talked a lot but we never talked about why I had left them. That, to this day, is the unspoken question between us. But at that time we were just content to be together and it seemed as if they had settled for a dad who just cared about them as best he could.

Ma was getting older and Dad, even though he still played his music, was beginning to lose his ear a bit and the notes were not quite as sharp as they had been just a couple of years ago. Sam was doing well and her family of three seemed to be thriving. Dor had two children and both she and her husband lived in Portarlington. Breda was also married and had two children and seemed to be making lots of money through buying properties, doing them up and selling them on. She always had excellent decorative taste.

'How are you really doing?' Ma asked me on Sunday evening after my boys had left.

'I hate this time,' I admitted. 'I hate to let them go. It tears me apart.'

'You need to stop thinking of yourself,' she told me. 'Material success isn't everything.'

'It's not the money, Ma,' says I. 'It's something inside me that just drives me. I can't help myself I want to be a perfect dad but I don't know how. Does that make sense?'

'You have to learn, son,' she told me. 'When you become a father you take on responsibility for another life. You have to fulfil that responsibility.'

'I will, Ma,' I promised. 'I will.'

The Monday was as boring as it was unsuccessful. It appeared that clients demanded the impossible and potential clients required miracles. I was not in the mood for diplomacy. My eyes streamed and my vision was blurred.

I picked up the phone to Julie. 'Have you managed to locate the Countess yet?'

'She's in London tomorrow. Arrives at Heathrow at seven in the morning.'

'Can you get me an appointment with her for the following day, and invite Professor Greenberg to the meeting.'

The Countess was as wildly gesticulating and dramatically dressed as usual. Her dyed blonde hair, immaculately coiffured to look as if she had just arisen from a passionate encounter, softened her piercing, pale blue eyes. The expensive cosmetic surgery knocked twenty years off her age. 'Darling,' she proclaimed, hugging me a little too tightly, 'you are the only man I long for.' She greeted Greenberg with a little less enthusiasm but with the formality given to someone you respect.

'Countess,' I began, 'I do not understand what it is you would like me to do for Professor Greenberg and his group.'

'It's simple,' she told me. 'You know La Contessa Juliana Le Grande.'

'If you say so, Countess,' I replied softly.

'I do,' she retorted.

'La Contessa has told me about a method of financing charitable projects like Professor Greenberg's. It is based on distributing profits from trading specialized financial instruments. I must say, darling, that it's all too complicated for me but I knew you could figure it out.' Professor Greenberg was happy to remain silent in the hope that something positive would emerge.

'I am not confident we can help,' I told the Countess, 'but we will use our best endeavours ...'

'So formal,' she sighed. 'These poor children need our help. Let's try our best. Okay?' I asked Greenberg to leave the room. 'You are not looking at all well,' the Countess remarked.

'Just a bad cold,' I assured her.

Silence.

'Countess,' I began, 'I am sure La Contessa Juliana would not involve herself in anything illegal but I did check with the Bank of England. They advise extreme caution with this type of proposal. In fact, they said that people who involved themselves in this type of business were usually a mixture of fantasists and fraudsters.'

'Really,' she exclaimed. 'I'm sure ... '

'So am I, Countess. As I said, I cannot see La Contessa being involved in anything that might be remotely shifty. But I think we should not get Professor Greenberg's hopes up.' We agreed that I would introduce Greenberg to La Contessa and leave it at that.

'My cousin Count Randolf would like to meet you,' she told me. 'I've told him a lot about you.'

'You are too kind,' I replied but I was barely able to contain my excitement. Count Randolf von Hatzenberg was an extremely influential financier. His blessing would convert our growing partnership into an institution— overnight.

'And what can I do for you?' La Contessa asked.

'I'm not sure, but there is a man I would like you to meet.'

She raised her eyebrows, 'Sounds intriguing already.'

Contessa Juliana Le Grande was thirty-six, blonde and very attractive. She had already gone through three husbands, one of whom was a Venezuelan finance minister. It was unclear how she had acquired her title but nobody ever bothered to ask.

I met Juliana six months earlier when I was conducting

business for a client in the Bahamas. I had stayed over the weekend and was relaxing with a Hemingway novel by the hotel pool. 'May I sit beside you,' she said as she pointed towards an empty lounger. She looked simply gorgeous.

'Sure,' says I.

'Champagne?' I offered.

La Contessa Juliana Le Grande told me her life story, explained how she simply loved Hemingway and offered me her undying friendship over a riveting two-hour, one-way conversation. I explained to her that I was in a committed relationship and she explained how boring this was for anybody. In the intervening six months we had handled two items of business for her and she had introduced three very valuable clients.

'His name is Professor Alexander Greenberg. He is a Harley Street paediatrician with an amazing vision.'

'Tell me more.'

'I'm afraid I cannot, Contessa. The Professor came to me for help and advice and I need to seek his permission first. What I did want to ask you, however, is this: if you were asked to support a project in Israel, would this cause you a problem?'

Contessa Juliana Le Grande looked angry. 'What do you take me for? A bigot?' She stumbled over her words.

'I am sorry, Contessa, I had to ask.'

'Mister Pey,' she continued, her left hand perched defiantly on her hip, 'I am a Jew. Not a very good Jew, I admit. But I am Jewish.'

'Thank you for sharing that with me, Contessa,' I began, 'this professor of mine is a very special man. I, unfortunately, cannot help him commercially. But your contacts might be prepared to get together.'

'I can't wait to meet him,' she smiled. Her 'on-stage' veneer was back in place.

By Wednesday my flu had disappeared and the blurring in my vision had corrected itself. Mimi kept telling me that I ought to see a doctor but now there seemed little point to that. It was two thirty and I was already half an hour late for my acupuncture appointment. I phoned ahead to make sure they could still fit me in. They could.

'I just feel so tense all the time,' I told Sergio. 'It's like the only time I relax is when I am lying here with pins stuck in me.'

'It's got to do with your sinus problems, no?'

'No. They've cleared up'

'Perhaps you need to slow down, not try to prove everything to the world all at once. You know, get pissed, do the things other people do.'

'I haven't drunk since college,' I told him.

'Why?'

'Because every time I drank I got drunk and I didn't like it.'

'It seems that everything you do, you do it to excess. Try having a nice glass of wine with lunch. It might work wonders.'

'Lunch?' I laughed.

'Yes,' he replied, 'the meal that comes between breakfast and dinner.'

'Dinner?' I quipped.

By four o'clock my schedule was so far behind that there was no point in trying to catch up. I rang Julie. 'I think I'll take the rest of the day off.'

'An American called Guy Henson is here. Says he was recommended to you by Andrew Patmore.'

'Make an appointment for him and ring Patmore. Ask him for background details.'

'He seems like a nice man,' Julie chuckled. 'He's offered me the Hope Diamond for a single night of passion,' she laughed.

'Already?'

'What do you mean *already*!'

'And you?'

'I wouldn't lend him money if that's what you mean. The rest is my business.' Julie was an excellent judge of character, but it was unlike Patmore to send a bad risk along.

I arrived at the office at eight the next morning and Professor Greenberg was waiting for me. 'Sorry to be so pushy,' he said, 'but I was telling my wife about you and she instantly liked you and thought you were the only person to help.'

'I am flattered, Professor, but your wife hasn't ever met me.'

The Professor touched the side of his nose with his right index finger. 'Oh, she knows,' he said, 'she knows.' I made coffee for the Professor and myself.

'As a matter of fact,' I began, 'I was going to ring you today. An acquaintance of mine, Contessa Juliana Le Grande, who currently resides in New York, would like to meet with you. I asked her if she could help, but naturally, I could not tell her of your plans. She is a good person, has many contacts in the right places, but most importantly, has lots of energy.'

The Professor looked hesitant. 'South American, eh?'

'Originally Cuban. Her family lost their gambling business during the Castro Revolution. They moved to Santiago where the good Contessa married and divorced very well.'

'Yes, but South America?'

'She claims to be Jewish, Professor,' I replied without acknowledging the implication of national stereotyping.

'That is not important,' he chided me. 'What is important is that she loves all children enough not to worry if they are Christian, Jew or Islamic. We are all God's children.'

'Precisely,' I replied. 'Just remember, South America also does not necessarily mean money launderer.'

I picked up the phone and rang the Contessa. She never got out of bed before noon and let me know how unhappy she was. But she agreed to meet with the Professor and to keep me informed.

I spent the remainder of the week in Switzerland looking after client interests, feeling very tired and constantly checking what I could and could not see. The blurring had frightened me. For the latter exercise I had devised an ingenious mechanism.

When I was in Ireland on one of my visits I had taken a photograph of the waterfall in Birr. I had the photo enlarged and I placed a black dot in the centre of the picture. Each day for the past week I would focus on the black dot and note the parts of the picture I could see without moving my eye. The verdant banks had all but been replaced by a greyness and the spire had vanished. I wondered if it had ever existed at all. Then, on a good day, it would reappear in all its splendour.

On the Friday I had arranged to meet Dieter Hendrick from Credit Suisse for lunch at the Metropolitan in Geneva. We had nothing important to discuss. It was simply a lunch in which each of us tried to find out what the other was doing.

'Wine, Monsieur?' the waiter asked. I hesitated.

'Why not? Dieter, perhaps you could order it?'

'But I thought you did not drink.'

'I don't, or rather, I didn't. But my acupuncturist thought it would be a good idea.'

'If you say so. But if I were you, my friend, I would change acupuncturists. Normally, these people have you drinking weed juice or suchlike and not the poison alcohol.'

But the acupuncturist was right. I did feel more relaxed after a half-bottle of wine, and I had another on the plane home and I swear it improved my sight. It was obviously getting rid of the remnants of my cold.

When I got into the office on the following Monday, I felt much more at ease with the world. I had decided to have a half-bottle of wine a day and since I had read somewhere that red wine helped reduce cholesterol, I decided it would have to be red wine.

There were a number of messages from the Contessa waiting for me. They said that I should call her at any time and I cursed not having contacted Julie over the weekend and for having ignored her calls for me to get back to her. But my life was just too full and I had used the time in Switzerland to get a few things sorted out in my mind.

'What time is it?' the Contessa moaned.

'Nearly nine thirty,' says I.

'PM or AM?' she snapped.

'Coffee time,' I replied.

'You are the only man in the world that I would allow to call me at this time,' she told me. Her voice changed mid-sentence from a moan to a purr.

'You are so charming,' I replied, 'but I am responding to your messages.'

The noise at the other end of the phone suggested she was getting out of bed. I got the feeling she was doing this so that a person beside her could not hear what she was about to say. 'Sorry for the delay,' she said finally. 'I needed to find some papers.'

'No problem.'

'I have met your delightful Professor and I have started to help. Tonight I have a friend of a friend of a friend; you know, someone with lots of money, coming to meet us. Can you be here, my darling?'

'Who is this person?'

'He is Spanish and his family own a bank in Spain and they are very rich.'

'Have you told him about the Professor's project?'

'Briefly. Just enough to get him on the hook.'

'Where and when?' I asked.

'The Dorchester at seven. I will meet you in the lobby.'

I agreed to meet Guy Henson for lunch at the Rugby Club in Hallam Street. Patmore's recommendations were normally good enough but I respected Julie's impressions.

He was a medium-sized man, with no real distinguishing features, and a laid-back Texan approach to life. 'How can I help?' I asked.

'I have a lot of oil interests,' he told me, 'and I'd like to cash in on my investments, so to speak.'

'There are many banks in Texas who could do this for you,' I told him.

'There sure are,' he said in a quiet voice, 'but I don't want half of Texas knowing my business before I do, if you know what I mean.'

'Wine?' I asked.

'Only if you are,' he replied. I ordered a bottle of St Emilion Grand Cru.

'Say, this is nice stuff,' Henson said. 'You sure know wines, mister.' I didn't. It was the most expensive on the wine list.

'Thank you. But I have to tell you that we are not experts in oil financing. I am surprised that Andrew Patmore couldn't help you. That is more his line.'

'Andrew who?'

My wine went down the wrong way. Patmore had spoken very highly of Mister Henson. 'I suppose we had better start at the beginning,' I spluttered. 'How did you find out about us?'

'I met a guy in Dallas who knew about you. He gave me your telephone number and hey presto.' He slapped the table.

'Can you remember his name?' I asked.

'No. He was a lawyer, I think.' Henson then explained that he wanted to raise money against his oil leases.

'How much, exactly?' I enquired.

'A hundred million,' he replied.

'That's an awful lot of money.'

'But I have the collateral,' he assured me.

I made an arrangement to meet Henson at the office at five thirty that evening and he promised to bring certified copies of the leases with him. I finished the wine and went back to the office.

At five thirty Henson arrived as scheduled. He opened his briefcase and emptied a pile of documents on to my desk. 'Oil leases as promised,' he declared.

'I brought someone along who knows a little about these things,' I told him. 'I hope you don't mind.'

'Not at all,' Henson agreed.

I left the room and returned with my expert. 'I would like you to meet Detective Inspector Cole from Her Majesty's Fraud Squad,' I said. Henson went pale.

'Ah, Mister Henson,' Cole said 'The last time we met I could swear your name was Reynolds.'

By the time I made it to the Dorchester, I was feeling quite tired. 'You look like hell,' the Contessa remarked.

'You look divine,' I replied, 'Fancy a drink?'

'I thought ...'

'Used to. Or more correctly, used not to. Decided to chill out instead.'

'I think we do business first, then have a drink, no?'

'Oh, okay.'

I followed the Contessa. She rang the doorbell to one of the suites and a sallow-skinned, heavy-set man with a dark greying beard answered the door. 'Tom, I would like you to meet Juan Miguel Laroza,' she said. 'Juan, this is Tom Pey, one of the cleverest deal-makers I know.'

'I am pleased to meet you,' the Spaniard said. He did not shake my hand. He bowed. Not too low, just enough to convey his superiority. I spent the next fifteen minutes outlining the Professor's plans.

'I do not wish to be rude, señor,' he said when I had finished, 'but I will do nothing to help Jews. How you say? I hate the bastards.' I felt a draining feeling in my solar plexus. I wanted to slap the man's face, but protocol and good manners dictated otherwise.

I rose. 'I am sorry to have wasted your time, señor,' I told him. 'I will see myself out.' La Contessa remained behind and since then I have refused to accept any of her phone calls, and I stopped acting for her or her clients.

In an odd way I could allow this Spanish aristocrat the luxury of hating a group of people for whatever reason he saw fit. What I could not understand was how this man could hate Jews and the children Greenberg was so desperately trying to help. What disgusted me was the probability that this was the man who occupied La Contessa's bed that morning.

I introduced Greenberg to a number of skilled fundraisers but I never learned whether the hospital was completed.

I was no longer the professional who cared about every detail. My work was becoming shabbier and clients began to notice. By winter of that year my client list had halved, and I had taken some unconventional decisions and my lunch-time drinking was obvious. Something had to give—and it did.

Chapter Four

London

March 1991

'Damn,' I swore to Julie, 'these glasses are not strong enough any more.'

'Old age, eh?' she jibed.

'Not me, babe. I was born old and am growing young.'

'I can make an appointment for you at the opticians.'

'No thanks. I'm going to Ireland next week and I'll drop in on my friend Danny McLaughlin in Athlone. He'll fix me up with a new pair on the spot.'

'We do have same-day service in London,' Julie joked.

'I know,' I replied, 'but that's supposed to be same-day service. McLaughlin does it as a favour. See the difference?'

'Men,' Julie sighed, 'spoiled brats the lot of you.'

It was raining when I reached Dublin Airport. I rented a car from Avis and drove through the Curragh, past Monasterevin and Mountmellick and called on Sam on the way. Kinnitty was a small, picturesque village about eight miles from Birr and was now home to Sam, her husband and their children.

'What has you over here?' she enquired.

'Came to see my boys and buy a new pair of glasses from McLaughlin.'

'He's a right one,' says she. 'I went to see him the other week and he gave me a new pair. Could spot a fly at fifty feet now.'

'Did he do them on the same day?'

'He did. But that was a special favour. He doesn't do that for everyone, you know.'

I smiled. McLaughlin could teach the best of us a trick or two about customer relations.

I met Danny the next day, and after exchanging pleasantries and enquiring about one another's general condition, he tested my sight. 'You need a new pair alright. Tell you what,' he announced, 'I'll run you up a pair in a couple of hours—on account of knowing you and all that.'

'I appreciate that Danny,' says I. I left Danny McLaughlin's feeling as if he was my friend and I spent the next couple of hours drinking coffee and planning a trip I needed to make to New York.

'How's that?' he enquired as he placed the glasses on my nose and bobbed from side to side like a hairdresser trying to get both sides of your hair the same length.

'They seem a little strange,' I told him.

'Ah, don't be minding that. Your eyes will get used to them in a couple of hours.' He was right.

The drive from Athlone to Birr brought back many memories. The rain thundered against the windscreen and the car bobbed and weaved through the undulating road. I had to slow down a couple of times to allow cattle and horses to cross the road as they searched for shelter.

I turned right at Kennedy's Cross and stopped outside Granny Pey's house. My Aunt had sold the place and it now lay in ruins; the thatched roof had rotted and fallen in. I felt no sadness because even in this decay the memories of my time spent there were warm in my heart. What did surprise me was the size of the apple tree to the back of the house. It was quite small. I had always thought of it as huge.

I spent the day at my parents' house and my boys came down to be with me. I showed them where I was born. It was now a supermarket selling newspapers and cooked chickens. Progress had gotten rid of the store where I weighed potatoes, measured gallons of paraffin oil and listened to tall stories from farmers who saw it as their duty to entertain while bargaining.

Next day I left around midday hoping to catch a five o'clock flight back to Heathrow. I decided to call on Dorothy in Portarlington as it was on my way to Dublin. As I left Tullamore and headed in the direction of Geashill, I noticed that the left-hand ditch seemed a bit wavy. Bloody McLaughlin, I thought. Him and his same-day service.

Then a man on a bicycle came into my field of vision. He was almost on top of the bonnet. I swerved violently and I saw him fall into a drain. Shit, I've killed him. I screeched to a halt and jumped from the car. Perspiration flowed freely down my back. My hands shook and my mouth was as dry as a sandpit.

'You all right?' I shouted.

Silence.

'Shit. Are you hurt?'

Groan.

'Thank God. Where are you?'

'Over here ya blind bastard,' the voice shouted. The man

was about sixty, rotund and balding. He was soaked to the skin.

'Sorry,' I started, 'I didn't see you.'

'Ya coulda killed me.'

'Sorry. Can I . . . ?'

'But ya didn't kill me. 'Cos nobody kills Jack Daly.' He was drunk.

'Can I drop you home, get a doctor or something?'

'Ya can drop me at the Thatch and buy me a couple o' pints if ya like.'

Jack Daly had a hollowed leg. He drank nearly ten pints of Guinness. I drank five and my hands were still shaking. But by the time we parted we were friends for life.

It was nearly six by the time I got to Dorothy's and I was in no fit state to drive any further. I told her what had happened as she prepared a bed for the night. 'McLaughlin knows what he's doing, Tom,' she told me. 'I'd go back to him and tell him what's happened.'

'Damn sure I will. I'll be on his doorstep first thing in the morning and I'll give him what's what.' The Guinness, the warm tea and Irish home cooking made me very sleepy and I slept through until seven the next morning.

I had enough time to reach Athlone by nine. Then I would ring Julie and have her reschedule my appointments for the day. Mimi wasn't very happy. We were due to move our furniture to our new home in Pluckley, a wonderful village in South Kent. Someone needed to be there when the furniture arrived that evening. I asked Julie to take care of it.

'I nearly killed someone,' I complained to McLaughlin.

He looked professionally concerned. 'Let me have a look,' says he. He placed the glasses under some sort of machine then checked my eyes again. 'Everything seems to be in order, Tom. I can't explain it. Tell me again what happened.' I told him about the wavy ditch and the man in the drain and how frightened I was. 'Mmm ... '

Silence.

'What are you thinking?' I asked.

'Don't know. It's beyond me, Tom.'

'What do you mean?' I asked.

'Come over to this contraption here and I'll try something out. You place your chin on the chinstrap, I'll flash a few lights and when you see one, click the button.' I complied. The test lasted about five minutes and when he stepped out from behind the contraption Danny looked concerned.

'Did it tell you anything?' I asked.

'I don't know how to say this, Tom, but I think you're losing sight.'

'For God's sake, Danny. That's no way to be joking around. All I want is a decent pair of glasses.' I hadn't told Danny about my flu or the photograph test.

'I'm not joking, Tom. I'm no expert but I think you're losing sight. I don't have the training nor the equipment to tell you any more. But I think you should see an eye surgeon immediately.'

'I'll find one in London,' says I.

'Immediately. Not next week.'

'Can you recommend anyone?'

'I've read about a Mister Daley in Harley Street. He's

pioneered retinal transplants. I'll try and get an appointment for you.' Danny came back about ten minutes later and told me that Daley would see me the next day. I rang Julie and told her to cancel tomorrow's appointments as well.

'Everything okay?' she enquired. The concern in her voice angered me and I hung up without answering.

Mister Daley put drops in my eyes and then looked at them through a telescope-type instrument. I will never forget the brightness of the light as it narrowed and elongated along my line of vision. I thought my brain would seize. 'It's serious, Mister Pey. It's very serious.'

'What do you mean?' I demanded.

'Unless I can get you the right type of help, you will go blind,' he told me.

'Shit.'

I apologized. 'I'm not one hundred percent sure of the cause of the problem,' he continued calmly, 'but the best man in the world is a chap called Rosenthal, Professor Ralph Rosenthal. I believe he's lecturing in California. I'm not sure if he will take you but I'll give it a bash.'

I sat in Daley's waiting room for what was only an hour but seemed like an eternity. Mister Daley emerged from his office. 'You're in luck, young man. Rosenthal is lecturing in Leicester and is practising at the Royal Infirmary up there. You need to get there for four this afternoon.'

'Thank you,' I said and extended my hand.

'Take a train, Mister Pey. Don't drive.'

The train from St Pancras arrived in Leicester at three forty-five and I took a taxi to the Royal Infirmary. The reception area was filled with sick people or people concerned about sick people. It looked grimy and I didn't want to be there. 'Doctor Rosenthal?' I enquired from a disinterested receptionist. She looked up a book. I wasn't impressed that she didn't appear to know one of the best eye surgeons in the world.

'Sorry, we don't have a Doctor Rosenthal. What department are you looking for?'

'The eye section.'

'Ophthalmology. That would be Professor Rosenthal.' The emphasis on 'professor' told its own tale. I was reassured. 'Follow the signs to ophthalmology. Oh sorry, are you able to see them all right?'

'Still able and hopefully will always.' She smiled.

'He's very good. He sorted my mother,' she told me.

I made my way along a warren of corridors and found a duty nurse who brought me to Professor Rosenthal's 'rooms'. It consisted of three rooms. The one on the left seemed to be filled with bulky computer equipment. The centre one, the one I entered, had wall-to-wall filing cabinets and an overfull secretary's desk. The one on the right was, by deduction, Rosenthal's. The glass half-door was ajar. I knocked and an American told me to come in.

Professor Rosenthal was a youthful middle-aged bearded man, abut six feet tall and wore glasses. He wore dark pants that protruded at the end of his lab coat. That was all I could make out because the professor was lying on his back on a consulting couch.

'Pulled a back muscle,' he explained. 'Just grab a seat and sit down.'

'Hi,' I began, 'I'm Tom Pey. Mister Daley sent me.'

'Daley not able to fix you, then?' He laughed.

'He said you were the best in the world.'

Rosenthal chuckled. It was clear he knew he was good. 'I'll get up in a minute. Can you tell me your symptoms.' I told him about the wavy ditches and the man in the drain. 'Suffered from many colds when you were growing up?'

'Well, yes.' I told him about my recent flu and my experiment with the photograph.

'Ever had major infections?' he asked.

'Not really. The usual, I suppose.'

'Okay. I'll need blood samples. Pass me the phone, will you?'

A couple of minutes later a nurse was rolling up my shirt-sleeve and jabbing me with a needle. I hate needles! Rosenthal got off the couch and straightened himself slowly. 'I'll need to do some tests and take a look at your eyes.' I agreed. This time the nurse put me on a drip. I was so terrified I began to shake. Rosenthal smiled knowingly. 'You'll need to stop worrying about needles. I won't let them hurt you,' he laughed.

The nurse smiled and I knew this was one promise Rosenthal couldn't keep. I continued to shake. 'We're just injecting you with a yellow dye. It's like the one they use to find leaks in drains. You might feel your temperature go up a little, but don't worry about it. I need colouring to take photographs of the back of your eye.' The very fact he told me made my temperature rise. I stopped shivering and the nurse patted my arm.

One hour later it was all over and Rosenthal guided me to his office. 'You got anyone waiting for you anywhere?'

'Julie,' I replied instinctively.

'Your wife?'

'No. Secretary.'

Rosenthal nodded. He knew the type but it didn't show in his face. 'You better let Julie know you won't be in work for a while.'

'Why is that?'

'If we don't operate in the next few days you'll be blind.'

'Fuck,' I whispered.

Rosenthal allowed sufficient time for the seriousness of my position to sink in. But I wasn't crying for my lost sight. I was crying because I arrived at this point and had nobody to hold me. I hadn't told Mimi where I was going or what was happening to me.

I rang Julie at seven. She was still in the office. 'Peter is going wild. He needs you in Geneva in the morning,' she told me.

'I'm taking a couple of days out,' I told her.

'You okay?'

'Let's just say I'm in the best hands in the world.'

'What's going on, Tom?' She was very concerned.

'I'm okay,' I told her quietly. 'I'll be fine. See you in a few days.' I hung up. I turned to Rosenthal. 'I'm in your hands, Doc.'

I stayed that night at a Holiday Inn. I didn't sleep a wink. I was afraid to close my eyes, afraid of darkness and of silence. I relaxed when morning came. At least now Professor Rosenthal could take over responsibility for my sight. It hadn't gone silently from me in the night. It would be fought for on an operating table in a couple of hours. I decided against ringing Mimi.

Rosenthal looked worried when I arrived at his office. 'How long have you had the symptoms?' he asked.

'A couple of days,' I told him.

'I just might, repeat might, be able to save your right eye. Your left one has gone too far already.'

I closed my right eye and looked through my left. 'I see fine through it, Professor,' I said quietly.

'It's gone, Tom. A couple of days at the most.'

'You mean I will see nothing through it?'

'No. I mean your central vision will be gone.'

'Central vision?'

'That's the part of the eye you use to see detail. To read. To see the colour of people's eyes, etcetera.'

'You mean I won't be able to read?'

'If we save your good eye you will. So let's be positive.'

The surgery wasn't as bad as I thought it would be. The only nasty bit was getting injected with anaesthetic in the eye. Afterwards I went back to Rosenthal's office.

'We'll know in a couple of weeks if the laser treatment has worked. We've treated a big area and we daren't do more today. But if it doesn't leak over the next couple of weeks or so, you have a fifty-fifty chance.'

'Leak?'

'You are suffering from a very rare disease for Europe. It is normally found in the central states of North America. It is called histoplasmosis. I suppose the best way of describing it is that your body has an immune reaction to an earlier infection. This causes blood vessels to grow in the back of your eye. These burst and you bleed into your eye. The resulting scars damage your vision.'

'Can it be cured?' I asked.

'If caught early enough the answer is yes. In your case it has progressed too far.'

'So what do I do now?' I asked. Professor Rosenthal told

me to take a few days off, rest and call him in the middle of the following week.

'I'll see you again in a month and if everything is okay we won't need to meet for a further three.'

'You will never go totally blind,' he told me as we parted. 'But if I can help it you will still have your central vision in your right eye. So relax and let's leave this in the hand of fate.'

It was nearly ten o'clock by the time I arrived at Pluckley. Mimi picked me up from the station and immediately noticed the bandage over my eye. 'What the hell?' she exclaimed.

'I've had laser surgery in Leicester.' After I had explained what had happened from the time I had arrived in Ireland, she vented her anger on me for not talking to her and letting her know what was going on in my life. 'I was too scared,' I told her. 'I just didn't want to believe this was happening to me.'

'And now it has,' she replied.

'Not yet,' says I. 'Rosenthal says it's fifty-fifty.'

'You need to tell Peter,' she told me.

'No,' I shouted. 'It's none of his friggin' business. Okay?' Silence.

'I need you,' I told her. 'This is the scariest thing that has ever happened to me. I need you to support me.' That night I slept in Mimi's arms and I felt safe.

Every quarter I went to Leicester to see Professor Rosenthal. Each time he took photographs of my eyes and each time he seemed pleased with the results. 'I'm glad to say,' he told me on the fourth visit, 'that you have had no reoccurrence for a year. Your chances now are very good. So let's say we step down your visits to twice-yearly but if you notice anything in the interim call me immediately.

I was going to miss this American. I am sure his relationship with me was purely professional but I thought of him more as a friend. He helped subdue my anger and to give me hope, and although I couldn't see as much as I used to and driving was a little precarious, I still managed a full and normal life. I had even begun to enjoy 'Neighbours' on the television!

Chapter Five

Geneva

September 1991

The Alps looked particularly spectacular as they towered above the blue, still waters of Lake Geneva. The breakfast at the yacht club caught its mood precisely, long slow and particularly delicious.

'Why do you want to sell your trust company?' I asked.

Pierre Le Trec was a small man with mean, unsmiling eyes. His face cracked in a grin. 'I don't need to sell it,' he told me. I hadn't asked him that question. I remained silent. 'I am going to retire. I would like to travel. See the world. You know, spend a little time.'

I decided he needed the money. The only questions I needed to answer today were why and how badly. 'How much?' My instinct told me to be very careful of this man. I relaxed, focused on a point in the middle of his forehead and concentrated. The little voice inside my head told me he would take a million dollars.

'Ten million,' he replied confidently. He saw my reaction. It was ever so slight but he saw it anyway. I needed to be even more careful. 'Not all at once,' he added. 'Say five million down and the balance over five years.' I laughed.

'Too rich for my blood,' I told him and poured a fresh cup of coffee. That was a mistake. He knew I was willing to continue to talk. I glanced at my watch. I couldn't see the face.

'Something wrong?' he asked.

'No. Just didn't realize the time. I need to be in London for a luncheon appointment.'

'You interested in Fiduciare Internationale then?' he asked.

'Half a million down and the other half a million next year. That offer is conditional on the books being satisfactory and you getting rid of any funny business before we send in the auditors.' He sipped his coffee but I gulped mine. 'I see you need time to think about it. Talk it over with your wife and get back to me. You have my number in London.'

'Can you do any better?' he asked.

'As the book says, Monsieur Le Trec, not a penny more, not a penny less.' Despite his protestations I knew when we shook hands to part that he would eventually accept. I needed to sweeten the pot, however. Not because I was soft or anything. But Napoleon was right—never leave wounded on the battlefield. They made the worst type of enemy. The difference in our styles was that Napoleon usually killed them. I preferred it if they were my allies.

By the time I got to Geneva Airport my sight had returned to normal. I could read my ticket and follow the signs to the departure lounge. Things were looking up. The sun was shining in London and the plane was going to depart on time. I rang Julie. 'Everything set for my lunch with Jim Fernworth?'

'One thirty at the Rugby Club.' I liked to take clients to the

Rugby Club. It was a private luncheon club that was run by a former England international. Everyone talked rugby and understood when not to intrude at tables.

Jim Fernworth was a loud New Yorker with a mission. 'I want Heinrich Holdings,' he told me, 'and I'm told you're the man to get it for me.' I feigned flattery. 'Heinrich is a Liberian-registered company. It owns substantial oil interests in Russia. But that is not what I want. I want the shares Heinrich holds in another Liberian-registered company called Tamworth Investments. This company is the owner of woodlands in Siberia.' I nodded. 'I'm prepared to pay fifty million dollars for the lot,' he said. 'That's a fair price.'

As an intermediary it was not my place to comment. I smiled. Fernworth didn't like this. The fifty million was designed to impress me. It didn't. 'You know Andrew Patmore well?' I asked.

'Just from business. He's a good man.'

'Us Celts usually are,' I told him.

'Yeah,' he agreed, 'you guys sure stick together.'

Later that afternoon I visited the offices of a well-known firm of accountants. I had a meeting with Jacques Le Feve, one of their senior partners. 'You chaps interested in acquiring gold certs?' he asked. Jacques was nearing his sixtieth birthday and was always on the lookout to make an extra few bob for his retirement. His deals hardly ever materialized but he was worth meeting on the off-chance.

'Who's selling?'

'A client.'

'Does the client have a name?'

'Yes.'

In addition to being a senior partner in a large accountancy firm, Jacques was also Swiss. I waited but in typical Swiss tradition, hell could have frozen first. 'You know this client?' He raised his left eyebrow and I knew he was going to lie.

'Long-standing.'

'Yours?'

He was becoming irritated. 'Why so many questions? Do you want to meet this client or not?' Under-the-counter deals happened quite legitimately, but they were often a front for money laundering. There was no question of Jacques being involved in anything illegal. But then if I was to meet the 'client', Jacques would be out of the picture and would rely on me making the correct choices.

'Give me photocopies of the certs and I will see what I can do,' I told him.

That evening I enjoyed a nice dinner at the London Yacht Club as Jacques' guest. Jacques talked about retirement and the need to put a nest egg aside to meet the refurbishment costs of his yacht. Jacques' idea of retirement was a one-hundred-footer in the Caribbean.

I was beginning to want the same things. Then I remembered Great Aunt Lil. *Why don't you feel jealous of someone less well off?* she was asking. 'Oh shut up,' I told her.

'I beg your pardon?' Jacques asked. He was both surprised and hurt.

'Sorry,' I replied. 'Not you. My Great Aunt Lil.' That confirmed it for Jacques. I was working too hard and the remainder of the dinner was spent advising me how to slow down. 'Tomorrow,' I assured him.

The next morning I checked in with Julie and told them I was off to Phoenix, Arizona, on a deal that had been going on for months and needed closing. I got Jacques to fax a

copy of the gold cert with a message 'Please arrange for
negotiation in Zug.' Julie would know what to do.

The connecting flight from New York landed in Phoenix at
noon local time. It was raining! I grabbed a taxi at the airport
and went to the offices of McClelland & Aesop, attorneys for
the potential vendors of the Liberian-registered group of
companies. The offices were plush and the blonde receptionist was expensively dressed. This was the type of place
where, if you had to ask how much the fees might be, they
already didn't want you as a client.

'I'm here to see Mister Farera,' I told her. Farera's office
was an edifice to ego. The solid oak panelling and thick, dark
green wool carpet complemented the solid brass nautical
accessories that screamed at you. I felt like I was in a sinking
ship and I wanted to jump overboard. Farera, a small, pudgy
man, sat behind a huge oak desk and beamed at me. He wore
a grey Italian suit and a top-of-the-range Rolex. His cufflinks
were diamond-crusted with emerald studs and his shirt
looked as if it had just come from the tailors.

'I act for the directors of Luscanne Investments,' he told
me. 'They might be induced to sell at the right price.'

'Sure,' I replied. I smiled broadly. 'But first we need to be
sure there's no mud in the sack, so to speak.'

Farera looked puzzled. 'Mud?' he asked.

'Sorry. Just an old saying from back home. What I mean is
that my client will need to be sure that any representations
your client makes are worth the paper and all that.'

'Naturally,' Farera agreed. So far, so good.

'We only want the assets. Shares in an offshore company
are rarely good value,' I told him.

Farera's tone changed. 'I don't like what you are implying, Mister Pey. My clients are unlikely to attempt to sell something of dubious value.'

'With respect, Mister Farera,' I replied, 'your client is a Liberian-registered company. Unless, that is, you would like to disclose the identities of the shareholders and for them to become parties to any agreement we might reach.'

Farera flushed. 'I was merely saying that …'

'I need to do the correct deal for my clients. Okay?'

'Sure.'

Farera gave me some information I needed on the background of the company. I would fax it through to London and hopefully they could make some real sense of it. What I had to establish was that Luscanne really owned the Russian woodlands and that this asset was free and clear—at least from all legal and registerable lines. The more nefarious ones would need to come out in the wash. That was where Kilbride came in.

Kilbride was a tall, skinny American who got on well with both sides of the Russian commercial divide. He was the sort of middleman who sold his services to both sides. Despite his lack of obvious morality, Kilbride took pride in delivering a quality service. His prices were high but they were worth paying if you wanted to do business and survive in Russia.

One of the things I always loved doing was walking. Whenever I arrived in a place I had never been before, I couldn't wait to drop my bags in the hotel, pull on an old pair of pants and some walking shoes and walk around like any other tourist. I loved visiting shops that sold local kitsch and I would come back with a case full of shaky snowmen, broken arrowheads and basketball caps that would say 'Bite me— I'm a Big Apple.' But I never bothered with photographs. For some reason I have always believed that our sweetest memories are captured in our heart.

That evening I walked through the heavy, humid rain through emptying street after emptying street and I got no flavour whatsoever of the local culture. I got back to the hotel at ten thirty. I hadn't realized that I had been walking for over three hours. It was early morning in London. I showered and rang Julie. 'You get my fax?' I asked.

'Passed it on to Mike Brandon. Peter thought he would be the best analyst to help you on this job. He has some experience of Russian commerce.'

'That's fine. Kilbride?'

'He rang earlier,' Julie replied. 'He left no message. He just said he would call tomorrow.'

'Damn,' I cursed. 'That means I'll have to spend another day here.'

'Would Mister Farera not come to London?' Julie asked.

Pause.

'That's not a bad idea.' I replied. 'Maybe I could get him to Geneva.' I doubted whether I could but there was no point talking any more to Farera without the information Kilbride would give me. 'Let me know what Kilbride has to say as soon as he rings.' I hung up and immediately rang Mimi. She was getting used to my trips being extended and I promised to make it up to her. That was over a dozen gifts I owed her.

The phone rang; it was Kilbride. A squint at the clock showed it was 5 A.M. 'Heinrich owns Luscanne Investments.

It's managed in Zug by your old friend Le Trec,' he told me. Although not the type of character a nice girl would bring home to her mother, you could take Kilbride's facts to the bank.

'Anything dodgy.'

'Not on the surface at any rate. SBC are named as bankers. They wouldn't handle anything dodgy.' I asked Kilbride to find out if there was any Mafia connection with the Russian asset and if so, how much. 'Ten thousand dollars,' he told me. I agreed to transfer his fee as soon as he gave me the information. I hung up and decided to ring the London office. The numbers were out of focus.

I rubbed my eyes but it only made matters worse. The room seemed darker. I wanted to pluck my diseased eyes out and trade them in for the ones I had before my Irish trip. I wanted to ring Rosenthal but I dialled room services and ordered a large brandy. I could always ring Rosenthal to-morrow. The brandy settled my nerves. Then I ordered a bottle of Barolo and called Farera. He agreed to meet me in Geneva a week later.

I rang Julie and got a flight home at eleven the following morning. That gave me enough time to drink another bottle of Barolo. 'God,' I prayed as I drank, 'I don't want to be blind. I'm just about to make it big time.' My fears dissolved in a heady mixture of belief in the Almighty and the calming effects of booze.

I arrived in London at eight in the morning and went straight to one of the airport restaurants for breakfast. 'Can you put a brandy in the coffee?' I asked the waiter.

'Scared of flying?' he enquired.

'Something like that.' I replied.

I studied the menu. I could barely read it with my right eye. I had known for months that my left eye was useless but I tried it anyway. The second Napoleon coffee quelled my sense of panic and I bought a ticket to Geneva to meet Jacques' client with gold certificates for sale. It wasn't until the plane had touched down that I realized I hadn't told Mimi what I was doing. I called Julie from the airport and asked her to take care of it.

I rang Rosenthal and made an appointment for the next morning. My meeting in Geneva was arranged for eleven thirty in the morning. That would give me sufficient time to meet Jacques' client, Robesbottom, have lunch, get back to Heathrow, catch a connecting flight to East Midlands and meet Professor Rosenthal first thing the next morning. Assuming I was finished with him by say eleven, I could catch a return flight to Heathrow. I could then pick up the documents Farera had promised to courier to London, study them and then talk to Peter. All in a days work!

Once I had shaken hands with Robesbottom, I knew I shouldn't be there but I decided to see the meeting through out of respect for Jacques. Robesbottom was a small, pudgy and ill-dressed man in his early thirties. 'How much are you selling?' I asked him.

'How much do you want?' he replied.

'We are talking gold, aren't we? I mean, not used cars or something?'

'I've got five billion,' he said as if five billion dollars was short change. I knew then why Jacques had failed to fax the certs to the office.

'Show me,' says I. He opened his briefcase and showed me a bundle of photocopied gold certificates in various denominations. They were all certified by a Swiss bank. 'Where are the originals?' I asked.

'In a Swiss bank,' he replied.

'In Geneva?'

'Zurich.'

'Why don't you trade with them?' I asked. It seemed a perfectly logical question.

'My client insists on a private placement,' he replied.

'Why?' I asked.

'His choice,' the pudgy thirty something year old replied.

'Are these genuine?' I asked.

'Of course.'

'Good. Then you won't mind coming to the Geneva office of the certifying bank. It will only take a few seconds. If they certify them then I will trade. If they don't, you will probably get out in say five years for good behaviour. Your call.'

Pudgy began to lose his composure. 'My client is a very private man and of considerable means,' he told me. 'Governments want to do him down. He is prepared to offer good terms for a private sale.'

'What did you do before you started trading in gold?' I asked.

'Insurance.'

'I'm going to be nice to you. If you promise to go back to your insurance business and only sell what you can stand over, I will forget we met.' I was going to forget anyway.

'They are genuine,' he assured me.

'There's hardly that much gold in the world, laddie. Take my advice and stay out of jail.' I left the Metropole and decided to downgrade Jacques' usefulness. I rang Le Trec and invited him to lunch. He told me he couldn't make lunch but would meet me at two.

During lunch I began to relax. For one thing I could read the menu with no problem. Secondly, I had a very nice half-bottle of claret to wash down a very passable filet mignon. I was even looking forward to meeting Le Trec. 'You thought over my suggestion?' I asked him.

'You mean your offer?' he replied.

'No. My suggestion.'

'I only consider offers.' His voice was brittle.

Silence.

'Stop playing games, Tom. You interested or not?'

'You're the gameplayer, Pierre,' I snapped.

'What do you mean?' he asked.

'Fernworth, Heinrich. Ring any bells?'

'I don't know what you mean,' he told me.

'Oh come off it, Pierre. You must have set this whole thing up.'

'I promise you, Tom. I am an honest broker wishing to retire.'

'Seems to me then, Pierre, as if you've taken on a client or two who don't share your moral fortitudes. Any Russian clients?'

I was fishing but Pierre wasn't sure how much I knew, if anything. He considered whether to answer or not. 'Would that make a difference?' he asked.

'I'm going to pass on the opportunity at this time. My partner would have a fit if he thought I would even consider buying something with a slight odour.'

'Take my advice. When you're cleaned up come and talk to me. I'd love to be involved but I need to be sure of what I am doing.'

'You will join me in a drink?' Pierre offered.

I looked at my watch. I had an hour and a half to get to the airport. I passed.

It was nearly nine in the evening by the time I got into the Holiday Inn in Leicester. My head was buzzing and I felt tired from the lunchtime wine. But I was sure of one thing. There was an underworld connection to the Russian woodlands and I would need to tell my client of my suspicions.

There was also a way that I could get Le Trec to clean up his act, acquire the asset for Fernworth and pick up the trust company for a song. I just needed my luck to hold out and that included my sight.

Professor Rosenthal injected me full of his yellow dye and photographed the back of my eyes. 'Fancy lunch?' he asked. 'It will give the picture boys time to develop your photos.' I agreed. We went to a little Italian place near to the hospital's Knighton Street entrance. It smelt of pizza and garlic. 'You're not looking so good,' Rosenthal remarked.

'Working too hard,' I replied.

'Is that all it is, Tom? You seem very pasty, off colour.'

'I'm fine Doc. Honestly.'

'Worried about your sight?'

'Not really,' I lied. 'What will be will be.'

'It's okay to be scared, Tom.'

'Stop preaching, Doc. I'm in the best hands. Okay?'

'You need to face reality,' he told me. 'Don't run from it.'

'I didn't realize I was.'

Silence.

'You fancy some wine?' I asked.

'Can't. You need my clear head this afternoon. Anyway, I thought your records say you don't drink.'

'Just the odd glass of wine. Nothing serious.'

'Just stop running, Tom. Reality is never as bad as the fear of it.'

'You setting me up to tell me something?'

'What I saw didn't look good,' he told me. 'I need the pictures to be sure. But you need to start facing the possibility.'

'What possibility?' I didn't want a reply.

'That you will become seriously visually impaired.'

'Blind?'

'In the technical sense.'

'You mean you can be a little bit pregnant?' I scorned.

'Let's wait and see the pictures, shall we?' I barely touched lunch but had two glasses of wine to steady my nerves.

Rosenthal studied the photographs. The silence was unbearable. 'Serious?' I asked. I hated the way I said it. I sounded pathetic.

Silence.

'For God's sake,' I snapped. 'Can't you tell?' Professor Rosenthal removed his glasses and looked at me. I knew he didn't want to say what he was thinking. He didn't enjoy this part of his job.

'We don't have the equipment here. You have a bleed close to the area of your central vision. It might be operable but I doubt it. I would recommend that you see a Doctor Fine at Johns Hopkins in Baltimore. They have the most accurate lasers in the world and Fine is an excellent surgeon. But you need to go right away.'

'What are the chances, Doc?'

'Not good. Less than fifty-fifty,' he replied.

'I've had worse odds than that, Doc,' I joked, 'and won.'

I found a phone and rang Julie. 'Get me a flight to Balti-more,' I told her. 'I have a piece of personal business to take care of. Before you ask, I'm fine.' I rang Mimi and told her something had come up and I needed to fly to Baltimore. 'How did your check-up go?' she asked.

'Okay, I think. He needs to do some more tests.' My sense of isolation was complete. I hung up and began to cry.

Chapter Six

Leicester
October 1991

By the time the flight lifted off from Baltimore I had decided I wasn't going to go blind. I wasn't certain how I was going to manage it but I felt sure that modern science would have an answer. By the time I had downed two swift Martinis I knew it wasn't an accident that I was in the business I was in. I could muster a number of investors and maybe find a cure for blindness.

I recalled a Dutch doctor I had met on my travels. He spoke of experiments in Switzerland where scientists were attempting to allow blind people to see by rewiring their optic nerves. My recollection was fuzzy. I wasn't sure if I heard the Dutch doctor correctly. I remembered that at the time I thought he was a crank. But then he brought me to Berne and showed me what they were doing. I wondered if they had progressed from that early stage.

The feeling of hope calmed me momentarily but then the panic returned. I decided not to tell anyone of my plight, especially Peter. How would he deal with it? Maybe he would be very understanding but kick me out anyway. I just couldn't take the chance nor did I want pity. Anyway, didn't Professor Rosenthal say that I would never lose *all* my sight? There is hope, I decided, I would just have to find a way of coping.

The arguments and counter-arguments raged in my head. I would have to tell Mimi. Maybe I wouldn't. I mean, would she still find a blind man an attractive proposition? Surely not. But then, she would notice, so I would have to take the risk and tell her and just hope she would stick by me. Then I thought of all the times I had chosen business over her. Panic. Now was her chance to get her own back just when I needed her.

My head felt like a washing machine, so I ordered two small bottles of wine to slow it down. By the time the plane touched down at Heathrow I had concluded that I would have to tell Mimi and take the risk.

It rained all the way from St Pancras to Leicester. I found myself a table in the first-class compartment and scowled at anyone who tried to occupy the vacant three seats at my table. It worked. I sat with my nose pressed against the window as the train passed emptied wheat fields. Now and again, lonely animals prayed for shelter from the driving winds. Droplets of rain ran down the glass then turned at right angles before disappearing towards the rear of the train.

The determination I had felt when I boarded the train turned firstly to anger then to hopelessness then back to anger again.

'What can you see, Aunt Lil?' I had asked her once.

'Nothing,' she laughed, 'but then there isn't much left worth seeing.' She chuckled.

'But you can't just see nothing,' I protested.

'Well I tell ya,' she continued, 'that's what I see—nothin'.'

'And what does nothin' look like?' says I.

'God, aren't you the eejit? Nothin' looks like nothin'. That's all.'

'Is it dark?' I persisted.

'Now don't be botherin' me,' she complained.

Silence.

I looked around the kitchen. It was obvious that poor Aunt Lil hadn't been able to see anything for a long time. Yellowed ashes formed a misty carpet under the table and a big cobweb clung undisturbed under the mantelpiece. The brass angels had browned in the smoke and her cat purred from the top of the opened flour sack.

'God,' I said finally, 'I can't imagine what nothin' looks like.'

Aunt Lil wiped her hands on her apron and then dabbed a tear from her eye with the corner of her apron. 'It's the most shockin' thing God could do to ya,' she told me. She sat down.'Ya don't see dark and ya don't see light. Ya just see the memories.' She wiped her face with her sleeve. 'But ya know what,' she said.

'What?' says I.

'God never closes one door but he opens another.'

I never asked her what she meant. Now I wished I had.

Professor Rosenthal looked genuinely disappointed and concerned when I arrived through the Knighton Street entrance to the Ophthalmology Department. 'Long trip?' he said.

'Long trip.' says I.

Silence.

'I thought I had beaten the damn thing,' he said. 'Just a one percent chance of reoccurrence.'

'You can't halt the march of fate,' I tell him. I didn't mean it. I wanted to scream at him, to tell him he hadn't tried hard enough or well enough. But I knew that was a lie too.

'Now we need to start the second phase of your treatment,' he told me. I sensed hope. 'If you are about to lose your sight, we need to give you the right equipment so that you can continue to do your job.'

'I don't want everyone to know,' I tell him.

'But you can't keep something like this a secret. People have a right to know. They'll begin to notice.'

'I have rights too,' I told him. 'I have the right to remain silent.'

The Professor knew he wasn't going to get much sense out of me. He had seen many people go through the shock of being told. All he could do was to let me come to terms with it. 'Take a few days off. Then come back and we'll talk,' he told me.

Silence.

'When will it happen?' I asked.

'Fine gives you a month at the outside.'

'How will I know?' I asked.

'One day you won't be able to read normal print.'

'Will it hurt?'

'Not physically. But you need to be emotionally prepared.'

'How can you be prepared for nothing?' I asked quietly.

Silence.

'You won't be totally blind,' he told me. 'You won't be able to read and . . . '

'And what?' I interrupted.

'You won't be able to see faces.'

'Like my kids?'

'Them and others.'

'My own? Will I be able to see my own face?'

I don't know why I asked the question. It was of no importance to me. Rosenthal didn't answer.

I rang Julie. It was great to hear her voice, her friendliness. 'Were you able to set up that meeting with Peter?' I asked.

'Tomorrow night. Seven o'clock at the Cafe Royal in Piccadilly.'

Pause.

'Don't snap my head off but are you okay? There's nothing wrong is there?' Julie sounded genuinely concerned.

'Nothing serious,' I lied. 'Just a few personal problems.' I hung up.

Loneliness is a cold feeling but the loneliness I felt was all the colder because it was self-imposed. It was as if I had an unfillable hole in my soul. I needed a drink badly.

The lighting at the Cafe Royal was subdued; the wooden panelling and highly polished mirrors created an ambience of a bygone era. Sophisticated hedonism. Peter was expensively but casually dressed. I always wore a suit. I saw it as my uniform.

Each month Peter and I met to discuss partnership business, fee income, potential new clients, any challenges and opportunities we faced during the month. We also used the forum to discuss difficult files we were handling. We tried to do this away from the office and I have to agree that our meetings were more open and useful because of the settings we chose. Every other month Peter or I would choose the setting for the meeting, and we tried not to go to the same place twice. 'Innovation develops ingenuity,' I once told Peter and we adopted it as a slogan for our business.

The waiter handed us the menus. I couldn't read mine in the low light so I waited for Peter to order. I would simply have the same. 'I can't see the menu in this light,' Peter told me. 'And I forgot my glasses to boot. Perhaps you could tell me what they have on.'

'Sorry,' I laughed, 'I can't see it either. Must be old age.'

'But you have your glasses in your lapel pocket,' he replied.

I fumbled and took my glasses from my pocket. 'These are my driving glasses. Useless for reading. Why don't we call the waiter and order from the specials?'

'Good idea,' Peter agreed. I relaxed. I told Peter about Le Trec. 'Sounds like you found a real artist. Any relation?' A pretty incisive judgement, I thought. We agreed to brief the client and declare our interest in the trust company. 'Seems like you know what you are doing,' he concluded.

The partnership was doing well. It was likely that we would go into profit that year after paying all salaries and expenses and Peter wanted to improve our IT infrastructure. I agreed. 'I would like us to assist clients acquire majority interests in companies that are underperforming. We could get in there, shake up the management, write new strategic plans and take a fee plus a small stake for our efforts,' I proposed.

'What are the risks?' Peter asked.

I spent the next two hours poring over my ideas and two very expensive bottles of wine.

'It seems it all hangs on us getting hold of that trust company. But we don't have the money for that.'

'No,' I agreed, 'but we don't need money. All we need is a lot of charm, a little genius and just a touch of luck.'

'Are you sure it's not the wine talking?' he laughed.

'You want in or not,' I snapped.

'We are partners,' he replied.

'Sorry I didn't mean it like that.' I then told Peter how we could take control of Le Trec's operation for nothing.

Ireland

End of October 1991

I touched down at Dublin Airport and knew what dying people meant when they said that there was a sense of closure in looking at something for the last time. My eyes drank in the emerald green hue, the creamy white overalls of the maintenance crews, the smiling faces of the Aer Lingus ground staff and the bustle of the capital city.

I travelled by train to Tullamore and Sam brought me to my parents' home in Birr. It was then that the significance of Rosenthal's words struck me. Soon I would not see my boys' faces. The best I could hope for was to know they were there; to touch them and feel them getting bigger and stronger.

I needed a drink to quieten the worm in my head that twisted my guts and stopped me thinking straight. I unscrewed the bottle of whisky I carried in my case and poured an extra large one.

I spent the day with my sons and I told them what was going to happen to me. I am sure they were concerned, but just as I was for Aunt Lil. My boys' concern was expressed as wonderment and this sense of disconnection from my plight made me feel even more cut off and lonely than before. Loneliness then gave way to unexpressed anger and frustration.

'What can you see now, Dad?' Adrian, my youngest, asked me.

'What will you be able to see?' Stephen wondered.

I didn't know the answer to these questions and I didn't want to find out either.

'It will be cool having a dad that's blind,' the younger one said.

Yeah,' the older one agreed. 'It's a pity you're not a

musician or something like that. Then you could be famous. Like Beethoven. He never heard what he wrote.'

'It shows,' the younger one chipped in.

I soaked up their images; their quick excited eyes, their long fingers, the parts of them that were me, the parts that were their mother.

I felt so proud to be their dad but such a failure that I lived in England and they lived in Ireland and even though we spent summer and Christmas and holidays together, it didn't seem enough. Now I was going to be of even less use to them. And when we hugged as I left for the airport, I hung on a little longer and a little tighter than usual. So did they.

The flight back was the longest trip I had ever taken. I reflected on my life up to that point and thought how pointless it all was; the excitement of my first job and the time Bob Hayes took to teach me the need to collect all the facts before making a decision, the importance Avon had placed on personal development and teamwork as a vital ingredient of running a successful business; the violence of Wall Street and the innovation required in my current job. It all seemed so pointless. All of it required one simple ingredient—the ability to see and read volumes of data and to assimilate it into coherent plans of action. I was going to be useless.

By the time I touched down at Heathrow I had reaffirmed my earlier decision. I would keep my sight problem a secret for as long as possible and I would use this time to accumulate as much money as I could. This would, at least, provide me with a nest egg for the future. But first I would need to visit Professor Rosenthal and get whatever help he could give me. Secondly, I was going to look at a building I had passed on a number of occasions but never stopped to really examine.

Amsterdam
October 1991

I don't know why the Red Pagoda near Schiphol Airport gnawed at me. I had passed it many times as I drove from the airport to or from various meetings. It was probably the fact that I had often wondered what went on there and had never taken the time to find out. Anyway, I was determined to see it even if it was the last thing I did.

I hired a car at the airport and drove along the motorway in the direction of the building. I began to panic. It didn't seem to be where I remembered it. But I persisted. Eventually I saw it in the distance and I slowed down and pulled into the emergency lane and stopped. Perplexed motorists hooted at me but I ignored them.

I got out of the car and looked over the protective barrier. The Red Pagoda stood proudly about a hundred yards away, just beneath the level of the motorway. I gazed at it in amazement for about five minutes before the stiff northerly breeze drove me back to the comfort of the car. But I was satisfied I had seen it and knew what went on within its red, majestic structure. It was a Chinese restaurant!

I drove back to the airport, handed in my car and checked in on my return flight to London. The check-in clerk told me the gate number and time of departure but I wasn't listening to her. I bought a cup of coffee and decided to check the monitors for flight details. I probably should have panicked but I didn't. The characters on the monitor were shrouded in a greying mist and I couldn't read them. It's happened, I thought.

It was as matter of fact as that. It had happened just like Rosenthal had told me and there was nothing I could do about it. 'Can you tell me the gate number for the British Airways flight to London?' I asked a passing stranger. He looked at me as if he was deciding whether to trust me or not. 'I can't read it,' I explained shyly. He gave me the information and went on about his business. That was the first time I experienced what it was like to feel separate. I wasn't sure if I would ever get used to it, and that scared me.

Leicester

October 1991

I explained what had happened to Professor Rosenthal. He tested my vision and confirmed what I had already known. The process of going blind had started. 'Just remember, Tom,' he told me. 'You will never go completely blind. You will get a grey line across your field of vision that will settle down in time and you will get used to it.'

'You mean blind doesn't mean blind,' I snapped.

'I prefer to say visually impaired. You can be registered as blind now.' This surprised me. 'You can't read the top line of the chart on the wall from a distance of six metres. This means you could be registered as blind. Your field of vision, we call it peripheral vision, is diminishing. This will continue. Soon you will not notice objects in your way and you will start to fall over them. So you need mobility training.'

'You mean a white stick?'

'Yes. A white cane or a guide dog,' he replied.

'A bloody dog?' I felt outraged.

'Not just now,' he conceded. 'The time will come when this may be necessary. I would give it about another six months or so.'

'What about reading?' I asked.

'You will need to use special magnifiers. These can be strengthened as your vision gets worse. Now you need about seven times magnification to read twelve-point print. Newspapers and telephone books will need much stronger magnifiers. But we can provide these for you.'

I considered this and immediately saw the problem. If I was to use this type of equipment in the office, everyone would know about my condition and that would be the end.

I told Rosenthal of my concerns. 'My advice to you is that you come clean with your employer. Most employers will help.'

I disagreed. Of course Peter would help but I didn't want his pity. 'I'll use them at home,' I told him.

'Right, then,' Professor Rosenthal sighed. 'I suppose I had better complete the paperwork to get you registered. This means you will get a lot of help through Social Services.'

'You mean go on a public register?'

'Yes. But you don't have to. It just makes accessing services much simpler.'

'No register. No Social Services. I will take care of myself.'

'That is your choice but I strongly advise against it. Your vision will change over the next few months and you need help to deal with it.'

'No register. No Social Services,' I repeated. He didn't push the point any further.

I was leaving Leicester with a small bag full of different types of magnifiers. 'Buy yourself a good desk lamp,' the Professor told me. 'One with anti-glare bulbs. Lighting is so important. The right light will make reading so much easier.'

'How bad will it really get?' I pleaded.

'Pretty bad. As I told you, you will need a white cane or a guide dog to get around, so you might as well prepare yourself for that.'

I shook his hand and thanked him for his advice. But I was determined to remain silent about my condition.

I asked Julie to set up a meeting with Pierre Le Trec and myself. Progress in both the requisition of the Russian real estate for Fernworth and the acquisition of the Swiss-based trust company depended on Pierre being truthful. The only way I could judge that was in a face-to-face meeting.

My sight, by this time, had deteriorated to the point where I could no longer see a person's eyes. This, in the beginning, seemed like a great handicap as I used to make many judgements about a person's character based on their eyes. I lived on the maxim that one's eyes were the window to one's soul, and believed that if your eyes were too small, you were probably devious. Similarly, if you had shifty eyes you were almost definitely not of honourable intent.

I wondered what my eyes looked like now. At one time they were clear and blue. Even though Mimi constantly reassured me that this had not changed, I was sure they were going to grey over like Aunt Lil's. 'The only difference is you look like you have just smoked dope,' Mimi told me.

'Eh?'

'You know? A little out of focus. It's like you're not focusing on the object you are looking at.'

So I had to develop a new technique of evaluation. I listened.

If you close your eyes and really listen to people when they are telling you something, you begin to hear the undulation of their accent, the timbre of their voice. If you really listen you can hear the slight pauses, the minute accentuation of words, the speed of delivery and how it changes minutely at different times during the conversation.

Everything I had ever learned about listening to music was now being used to listen to people. Everything that had been instinctive about the way I heard my Dad play and how I subsequently translated that into the rhythm of dance was now being focused on interpreting a person's intention from the way they spoke.

I rang Julie and asked her to get me an appointment with Le Trec. Five minutes later she rang me back. 'Le Trec is on holiday with his wife,' she told me. 'I managed to contact his ship and he'll meet you in Miami on Monday next. I've already booked the flight.'

My working days were now an almost twenty-four hour affair. I could no longer read normal print, even with nine times magnification, so I had to bring all my work home and Mimi would read it to me in the evenings. When I was travelling I would use the excuse of being away from the office and ask Julie to read my mail and reports over the phone to me.

The real crunch came when I had to sign contracts. I could just about get away with it when there were no questions to be answered on the contents of the document. But as soon as somebody would say, 'Are you happy with the format of Clause 5?' I was beggared.

What I used to do was flip through the pages, look blankly at the back page as if deciding on whether or not to sign. 'Mmm. Let me think about it. I'll let you have it back to-morrow.' I knew this frustrated the hell out of people who had worked hard to complete a transaction, but there was nothing I could do about that. Was there?

Mimi dropped me at Heathrow on Sunday morning to catch a midday flight to Miami. She insisted on bringing me to the check-in desk despite my protestations to the contrary. 'You're not safe,' she told me. 'It's time you started facing up to your responsibilities. You are not the only person in the world, and if something happens to you, an awful lot of people will be affected.'

'I'm alright,' I insisted and I snorted through my nose to ward of any more homespun truisms.

'He can't see too well,' Mimi told the check-in clerk. I wanted to explode with rage.

'I'll get somebody to help,' the clerk replied.

'I'm not blind,' I insisted but neither the clerk nor Mimi listened to me. I knew that they only wanted to help but it seemed to me as if in their rush to do the best they could for me, they had forgotten about moi. I wasn't about to let that happen. 'If anybody lays a finger on me,' I warned, 'I'll sue for assault. Now, what gate does the plane depart from?'

The check-in clerk hesitated. 'You'll take the assistance these people offer,' Mimi warned. 'You're like a child that decides they don't like spinach before they've even tasted it.' She turned to the clerk. 'He'll accept the help,' she told her.

About five minutes later a gushing and rather camp member of the ground crew came to bring me to a point where I could wait. 'Somebody will pick you up from here,' he told me, 'and assist you in boarding.' I didn't bother to thank him.

I sat in a small, seated enclosure surrounded by cripples and elderly and I began to feel revolted with myself and with them. There was no way I was going to be a bloody defective and that was that!

'Mister Pey?' a female voice called. I stood up. 'Hi. My name is Minette and I'm going to help you board your flight. Would you like to take my arm?' There are some advantages to blindness, I thought!

Le Trec was on route from Florida to the West Indies and we met at the Hilton near Miami Beach. Pierre looked a little perturbed at having to interrupt his holidays to meet me and told me so. 'It's important,' I told him.

'Go on,' says he.

I told him about Fernworth and his interest in the Russian real estate. Pierre disguised any hint of surprise. 'You own Heinrich Holdings,' I told him. 'It owns the woodlands.'

'How did you learn this?' he asked. He was not annoyed at my intrusion into his affairs, nor surprised at my knowledge. He was simply interested.

'You know a Mister Farera?'

'Yes.'

'He's selling Heinrich for you.'

'So why not buy from him?' Pierre asked.

'Because I'm dealing with you. How much?'

'Two point five million dollars.'

'That includes the trust company?'

Pause.

'Yes. But only if the deal is cash.'

'Paying for it won't be a problem,' I told him. 'Establishing what we are buying might be a little more difficult.'

Pause.

'Any, em, insurance premiums outstanding?' I asked him.

'One point five million,' he replied.

I whistled. 'We might just be able to complete the deal when you get back off holidays. In the meantime get Farera to cool his heels.'

That evening I tried to stroll along the beachfront but the alternations of light and dark confused me. I stumbled over up-kerbs and I bumped into a lady who hurled abuse at me and asked me if I was blind. Even though I had only wandered about five hundred yards from my hotel, the greatest pleasure I had derived from travelling was now no longer available to me. I spent the rest of the night in my hotel room drinking. I can remember trying to cry, but I could only muster anger.

By the following Tuesday I had tracked Fernworth down. He was in Dallas and on his way to Beijing. I told him everything I knew about Pierre, Heinrich, the trust company and the money owing to the Russian Mafia.

'What are you asking me?'

'You pay the two point five million for the Russian property and we get the trust company for free.'

He hesitated.

'Two million.'

'Two point five million and we'll manage Heinrich for free for two years.'

'I'll get my lawyers on to it straight away.'

That was what I liked about wealthy businessmen. They knew what was important and they got it but they always left a little for the small guy who could help them. Now I had to convince Peter.

We met at Langan's and I ordered the specials. 'They sound delicious the way the waiter describes them,' I told Peter. We went through the usual partnership business and we were doing well. Our efforts were now paying dividends and Peter seemed very pleased.

I brought him up to speed on the Fernworth deal. I told him we were picking up the trust company for nothing. 'Sounds good,' he replied. I resented the lack of enthusiasm in his voice.

'Good,' I exploded. 'It's bloody miraculous.'

'I'm not saying you haven't done well,' Peter replied. 'But I am concerned.'

'Concerned?'

He didn't flinch at my anger. 'It's you, Tom. You've changed.'

'Changed?'

'Yes. Changed. For one thing you are drinking far too much and for another your decisions are becoming interlinked.'

'What do you mean, drinking too much?' says I.

'See what I mean,' he replied. 'I would have expected you to try and discuss your decision making.'

'That's business,' I spat. 'Drinking is personal.'

'And we are friends?' he asked.

'Yes.'

'Then as a friend, please quit before it's too late.'

'I will, I lied.

He then went on to tell me that I was beginning to construct deals like a house of cards. 'Each outcome gets invested in the next opportunity, and so on. The problem is if any one outcome fails to materialize, the whole chain collapses and we will have ended up investing a lot of time for no return.'

'Am I not the biggest earner?' I retorted.

'Far more than I,' he replied, 'and I realize that. But it's like you are desperately trying to be in control of a hundred events all at once. I've seen this before and it's normally a forerunner to burnout.'

'Burnout!' I snorted.

'Is there something bothering you?'

'Nothing,' I replied indignantly.

'But it's clear that there is something bothering you.'

I reached for the bottle of wine the waiter had left earlier.

I hit it with the back of my hand and it spilled on the table-cloth and down Peter's trousers. 'Shit,' I spat.

'Calm down,' Peter urged. But I got up from the table and walked quickly towards the entrance. On the way I walked into an ice-filled bucket containing a bottle of champagne. The whole thing splattered across the floor. I panicked and began to cry and the waiter brought me to the door and put me in a taxi.

'You'll be okay in the morning, sir,' says he.

'If only you knew,' I replied.

There is something about secrets that eats away at a relationship like a cancer. Julie had asked me on more than one occasion if there was something wrong with my eyesight and if I should have my eyes tested. I always reacted with an angry denial and a stiff warning to her that she should mind her own business. Conversation between Peter and me became stiff and lacked the candour and cordiality that was the hallmark of our previous business relationship.

The London office continued to flourish and business people from all over the world flocked to it to discuss their ideas or to use our expertise in either opening doors, financial engineering or, since the acquisition of the trust company, introduction to its many services.

Pierre continued to manage the trust company for us and we had weeded out some of his old clients for whom we could not obtain first-class references. Within six months Fernworth was drilling successfully on the Russian property and he was recommending new clients to us.

As the trust company grew over the following twelve months, the trustees made many investments on behalf of their clients in numerous private limited companies, mainly in Europe and the United States. Peter and I advised the trustees and took on turnaround management in some of the newly acquired companies. We were into business that spanned agriculture to television and radio production, and my life at last seemed to be fulfilled, except for my blindness.

By now I could no longer move around anywhere except in places with which I was familiar—like home, the office, the Rugby Club, Victoria Station and the Bakerloo line from Regent's Park to Charing Cross. Charing Cross mainline station was also not a problem and I knew exactly where the Railway Bar was located.

'You ought to tell Peter,' Mimi told me one evening. 'He has a right to know.'

'He only has a right to know what I want to tell him,' I spat.

I polished off the bottle of Barolo I had started and went to bed. Mimi followed me into the room. 'At least tell Julie,' she coaxed. 'She'll be able to help you in lots of ways. She could read to you or cover for you with clients.' This made perfect sense to me. Julie was not the type of person to break a confidence.

Next morning I spilled the beans to Julie. 'I've suspected for some time,' she told me. 'But you need to tell Peter.'

'You mustn't tell anyone else,' I insisted.

'But the poor man is worried sick. He knows you are keeping something from him and I wouldn't be surprised if he thought you were working deals for yourself.'

'Me? Moonlighting?'

'If you told him the facts, Tom, he'd be relieved.'

'He's not to know. That's final.'

My day-to-day working improved over the next three

months and the amount I drank lessened in direct correlation. But the tension between Peter and myself became palpable.

One day the inevitable happened. Peter snapped.

Peter rang me at home one Sunday evening and asked me to take care of a client for him because he had to go to Vienna on urgent business. 'This man is the eldest son of a man who was my father's best friend. They were both in the diplomatic service together and all that. The families have remained close ever since.'

I knew what Peter was telling me. This was important for him and his family, so I should stay off the drink and be a good boy. I agreed. I met Karl von Brug at the Dorchester and I ordered the same as him. 'Wine?' he asked.

'Be my guest,' says I. I waved my hand majestically and the wine waiter arrived. Karl ordered a snappy German number and we relaxed into easy conversation. I waved my hand again and another snappy German number arrived.

Then the inevitable happened. I spilled my glass of wine because I knocked it over. Karl thought I was drunk and politely excused himself. I was left to pay the bill and had to get the waiter to place his finger in the spot where I needed to sign the credit card slip.

Next morning Peter thundered into my office. 'I have had enough,' he shouted. 'Unless you tell me what is going on, I'm going to dissolve this partnership.'

'Dissolve it,' I snapped, 'I'm out of here.'

Julie came in after Peter left. I told her what had happened. 'Tell him the truth,' Julie pleaded.

'Tell him nothing,' I snorted, 'I'm off for a nice cool bottle of champagne.'

'It's nine thirty for God sake. You can't disappear inside a bottle for the rest of your life. Thirty employees depend on you. You have been given a gift to turn ideas into workable solutions and a lot of people believe in you. Are you simply going to turn your back on them?'

'Fuck them,' says I. 'I'm thirsty.'

It took about six months to wind up the affairs, and Peter and I met a number of times during that period. The great friendship and trust that we once had for one another was replaced with anger and suspicion although I suspect Peter felt bewilderment and a sense of pity for me. Our words were always tense, to the point and lacked enough caring for argument.

Peter had decided he'd had enough of business and suggested that perhaps business had seen enough of me. I agreed with him. 'What will you do?' I asked him one day.

'One of the things I really admired about you,' he told me, 'was the way you listened to a person's idea and then you motivated them to go even further with it. I'm going to take advantage of what you taught me and put it with what I knew and use it to help others. I'm going to work in the international voluntary sector and bring forward some of those great ideas that get buried because they have no champion.' I nodded my approval. 'What about you?' he asked.

'Don't know,' says I.

'If only you didn't drink,' he told me. 'I know it's only because of something inside you that's boring away at your very soul. I'm only sorry that I wasn't a sufficiently good friend to be able to help you. Just so long as you know I would have helped if I knew how.'

'I know you would,' I replied. 'But maybe nobody can help me.'

'It's usually the case,' he began, 'that nobody can help us unless we are prepared to help ourselves.'

Peter and I shook hands over the packed cardboard boxes of files that once pulsated with the excitement of commerce. Now they were pieces of paper to be tallied by accountants who presided over the dismemberment of our aspirations.

I never met Julie again although she did send me one Christmas card:

Found a new job.
The boss drank so I'm looking again.
Happy Christmas.

Love Julie

Chapter Seven

I spent another six months doing odd jobs for old clients but this work soon dried up. Gone too were the old connections in New York and the City as news of my drinking spread through my circle of friends. Andrew Patmore still took my calls, was still polite but knew better than to risk any of his contacts on me.

The amount I drank reduced steadily over this time as the pressure of getting around lessened. I hardly ever went out and when I did it was usually at weekends and Mimi was with me. During this time she never complained about my not working, but now and again I would dismiss her comments about me 'growing into myself' and 'looking depressed'.

'Not me,' says I. 'Like all Paddies, I'm hard.'

She would never argue.

Each evening I would sit at table unshaven and in clothes I had slept in all day and I would open a bottle of wine with great delight. 'Next week,' I would tell her, 'I'm going to do something really exciting. I'll ring up Patmore and get him to invest in a film script idea I have. What do ya think?'

Mimi would smile encouragingly.

I am glad I could not see the pity in her eyes. I don't think I could have taken that.

But I babbled on from week to week, my stories of future successes becoming even more grandiose, my grip on reality becoming ever more tenuous. I was becoming more and more lonely but I no longer possessed the sensibility to recognize it, I drank so that the hole in my soul could be filled.

At first unemployment seemed like a perfect opportunity for me to have a fresh start and I was no longer fettered by the need to satisfy the demands of the wealthy. I was free to choose the job I wanted and go for it. Then I convinced myself that I would have no problem getting a job. But then, who needed one anyway? I was far above working for somebody else.

Hadn't I planned, run and successfully turned around many businesses? Hadn't I built up the partnership single-handedly? Wasn't I a member of Mensa? That was sufficient proof of my genius. All I needed to do was to figure out how to handle the fact that I couldn't see. Not from an emotional sense. I really couldn't care less that I could no longer see. It was simply what would others say or think? 'I know,' I thought. 'I'll see Rosenthal. He'll know what to do.'

I grabbed a train to Leicester and polished off four large gin and tonics on the way up. By the time I got to Rosenthal's rooms he had gone home. 'I don't seem to have an appointment for you,' his secretary said. I got very indignant and told her about the scandalous levels of efficiency in the National Health Service. 'I can give you an appointment at eleven tomorrow,' she said, anxious to avoid a row at six o'clock on a Tuesday evening. She was due to knock off at five.

'I suppose I'll have to settle for that.'

That night I checked into the Holiday Inn. About fifteen minutes after I had settled in the room the phone rang. It was the manager. 'I'm sorry, Mister Pey,' says he, 'but your credit card doesn't seem to have gone through.'

'No probs,' says I. 'I'll give you another one.' That one went through and I explained to the girl at the front desk that I had just come back from a long trip to Venezuela and I hadn't had a chance to pay the credit card bill yet.

She nodded politely.

That, I thought, would also explain my crumpled suit, and unkempt appearance.

I looked even worse the next day because I had not brought any overnight bag with me, so I wasn't able to shave or even comb my hair. I explained this to Professor Rosenthal, who took notes and only made understanding comments. He checked my sight and sat me down in a chair in his office. 'You are blind, Tom,' he told me. 'That fact hasn't changed from the last time we met. What has changed, however, is that your sight has gotten worse. It still has a bit to go but you should now go on the Blind Register.'

'What caused it?' I asked him.

'As I told you before, an infection you had some time ago.'

'Yes. But which one?' I persisted.

He talked me through my childhood infections but he thought none of these would be the cause. Then I told him about falling off the roof and banging my nose on the tree and the subsequent blood poisoning. 'That could very well have been the cause,' he told me, 'but there is no way of being absolutely certain.'

'A chance in a million,' says I.

'These things usually are,' he replied.

'Bang! You're dead,' says I.

'I beg your pardon,' says he.

'That's what Jimmy said when he shot me,' says I.

'Tragic accident,' says he.

'I wish I was,' says I.

'You wish you were what?' he asked.

'Dead,' says I. 'I wish I was dead.'

Professor Rosenthal told me of the help I could get and how I could function almost normally despite my disability. 'But first you have to stop feeling sorry for yourself. When you get back to Bromley you should also register with the local job centre. They can help you get back to work and they'll provide you with the necessary equipment for you to do your job.'

Slowly but surely reality was beginning to set in. Not only was I blind but I was unemployed, and if I had any chance of living a normal life I would have to get a job. I also began to realize that having a grip of reality was becoming an intermittent occurrence with me and that the intervening periods were becoming more Walter Mitty–like.

Rosenthal relit a flicker of hope inside of me and I left with a determination to get back on a track that represented some semblance of normality. I agreed to allow Rosenthal to register me as a blind person. My disability was now official and could no longer be denied. I rang the Bromley job centre as soon as I got back from Leicester and was told to come in for an interview on the following Monday morning.

I didn't drink over the weekend and I duly turned up on time, smartly suited and booted. I was ready for business and I aimed to show them that this was the case. I sat in a line with others who, like me, were looking for a job. About an hour later my name was called and I went forward to

meet a young girl who sat behind a desk. 'Have you filled in
your form?' she asked me.

'What form?' says I. She said I had to fill in a form and she
called out its number. 'No,' says I. 'But I can't.'

'Why not?' she asked gently.

'I can't see it,' says I. This was the first time I had admitted
my little problem to anyone other than Mimi and Julie.

'Do you have a sight problem?' she enquired.

'Yes,' I whispered.

'Are you registered blind or partially sighted?'

'Blind,' I whispered. She wrote it down.

'I'm sorry,' says she, 'but you're in the wrong place. You
need to speak to our disability employment advisor.'

'Oh?' says I.

'I'll make an appointment for you,' she offered.

My appointment was for the following day. I left the
job centre totally clear that I was different and that this
would always be the case, even amongst the ranks of the
unemployed.

Wendy Craddock was a small, petite lady of unbounded
optimism. She assured me that she was with me all the way in
my quest to get a job and she set about helping me to identify
suitable opportunities. Wendy explained that I would have
to read the newspapers and professional magazines and
select jobs from these. Then I would need to apply.

'How can I do that?' I asked.

'Have you anyone who can read for you?' she asked.

'Yes,' says I, but secretly my heart was sinking. Disability
was meaning even more dependency for me and I didn't
like that.

'You will also have to disclose your visual impairment to employers,' she told me.

'Why?' says I. 'It doesn't affect my brain.'

'If you can convince employers of that, you won't have a problem getting a job. What type of job are you looking for?

'Financial director of a public quoted company or equivalent,' I replied confidently.

Wendy hesitated. 'Perhaps I could write down "accountancy work"?'

'Fine,' says I.

'But you go for it,' she urged. 'There's no reason why you can't be exactly what you want to be.' I felt reassured by her confidence. 'I will meet you as often as I can,' she told me, 'and anything I can do just let me know.'

Over the next month I studied the job advertisements in the *Times*, *Financial Times* and professional magazines. During that time I applied for only one job—financial director in a medium-sized listed company. The industry and scope of the job appealed to me. I didn't get an interview—people with more relevant experience had applied! This didn't dent my confidence. It simply caused me to double my efforts.

I rang Wendy. 'I've decided to widen my scope,' I told her. 'I have a lot of relevant management experience so I will try general management posts as well.'

'You keep trying,' she told me. Nothing in her voice led me to believe that my aspirations were anything but reasonable. I spent the next two weeks getting my CV in order. I visited one of London's top employment agencies and met with one of their chief consultants, who began by rewriting my personal profile.

'I want to portray myself as a dynamic individual with a

sound management and financial background. 'I suppose,' I continued, 'I could be thought of as a bit of a visionary.'

He seemed impressed. 'Anything else?' he asked.

'Well, yes,' I hesitated, 'I've got a slight visual impairment.'

'I see,' he replied. 'How slight?'

'I'm registered blind.' His enthusiasm waned as he saw the possibility of a quick finder's fee slip from his grasp. 'Is that a problem?' I asked.

'No problem,' he smiled.

Armed with my professionally prepared profile, I began to apply for jobs in earnest. During that month I sent out nearly one hundred applications and I received not a single letter of acknowledgement in response. I was infuriated and could barely catch my breath when I spoke to Wendy.

'I didn't want to dampen your enthusiasm in any way,' she told me, 'but we find that getting blind people a job is the most difficult thing we have to do.'

'But it's not impossible?'

'It's difficult, Tom,' she admitted.

'But not impossible?' I enquired.

'You go for it,' says she. 'I'll do everything I can.' I knew she wanted me to succeed, if only to restore her confidence in human nature. But above all else, Wendy was a realist.

Andrew Patmore and I remained good friends despite the fact that I was no longer in the business. I told him about my difficulty. At first he was shocked and then he was angry that I had never told him before. He made it clear to me that he considered himself a friend but now he wasn't so sure. I apologized.

'Well Tom,' he told me, 'would you hire a blind man?'

'But I'm not blind,' I told him angrily, 'I can still see.'

'Aye, but how long for and how much?'

'For as long as I can,' I snapped. 'And I can get all the equipment I need to help me.'

'And that's the problem. What would shareholders do with a blind chief executive or financial director?'

I was stumped. 'So, I shouldn't try to get a job then, just sit at home and drink myself to death?'

'Maybe you could lower your sights a wee bit,' he advised.

'You mean a blind janitor would be acceptable?'

'I mean that there is nothing to be gained from failure. Nor is the answer to be found in a bottle of Nuits St George.'

For the first time since I had joined the ranks of the unemployed I felt the cold chill of commerciality bite at my ankles. Being unable to see properly did make me different and that difference was trying its best to keep me out of a job. My determination to succeed was slowly being replaced by an irresistible urge to get pissed out of my brains. I did.

London
January 1993

I had made nearly three hundred applications for various jobs, none of which resulted in an interview. Unemployment now became a condition that ensnared me. 'Tomorrow I will get a job' progressed to 'tomorrow I will understand the system and get maximum benefit from it.' Then came the phrase 'I'm useless and I'll never work again.'

I continually oscillated between the early and late phrases as job application after job application was unsuccessful. Call me a slow learner if you will, but three hundred job applications later, I had not had a single positive response. I decided on a little experiment.

I prepared a batch of ten applications all for senior positions. This time I left the B word off my profile. It worked! I got three requests to attend interview. I do not blame these three employers for not hiring me. After all, I had been dishonest on my application to them and blindness is easily discoverable. But I do have serious questions about a disability system that only sees the 'dis' and not the 'ability'.

Similarly, by focusing solely on the 'un' and not the 'employed', then the cancerous condition of unemployment becomes chronic, with a cavernous slide to hopelessness and to feelings that one is the lowest of all humanity. I didn't want despair to grip me, but I was losing the battle.

I unloaded my complex feelings on Wendy. 'I think you're depressed,' she told me. Those words lifted a burden from my shoulders. I wanted to agree with her but I equated depression with failure and I wasn't going to admit to failure.

'Depressed? Oh, I don't know. I've applied for nearly three hundred jobs and ... nothing.'

'So what do you expect?' she chided me. 'You need to accept your visual impairment and then get on with life. Accepting that you are blind means accepting that your old life is gone forever.' She didn't pause for breath. 'I'm going to send you on a course to Dorton College in Sevenoaks. It's a great place.'

'What kind of course?'

'A rehabilitation course.' She said it in a way that left me with no argument. Like it or not, I was going on this course. That was the way Wendy was.

'Rehabilitation?' says I.

'Yes. It will help you cope with your sight loss. Then when you get back, we'll see about getting you a job.'

Sevenoaks, Kent
July 1993

Beyond the church-like, brown-bricked students' lounge lay a grassy quadrangle which was more reminiscent of a postmodernist Stalag than a place of serious rehabilitation for blind people. The flowerless lawn was surrounded on four sides by steel posts supporting canopies that added a Wagnorian finality to the utilitarian buildings which housed our bedrooms. Indeed, by the time I had made it to my room I had changed my mind about what was called the students' lounge. I now wondered if it was fitted with shower heads!

The bedroom itself was minimalistic and set out in pine. My room had two windows as it was a corner room, and against the south-facing window was a small pine desk. On the north-facing wall was a wardrobe and my bed would have paid adequate homage to the penitent monks of the Middle Ages. I longed for the comfort of my own home.

By next morning all the rehabilitants had arrived. There were six of us in all. Joan, a South Kent housewife with three children, who had recently begun to lose her sight through a medical condition. John, a 27-year-old, high-flying sales executive who had lost his sight as a result of a head injury he sustained in a car accident. Brian, a guide dog owner with some limited vision; he told us he was born that way. Willie, a totally blind man who had never seen the light of day in his life and whose ambition it was to learn how to use a computer. Spencer, a young man of 25 who was losing his vision. He suffered from retinitis pigmentosa. Finally, myself, a disgruntled individual in need of an identity. A bunch of no-marks, I thought.

The staff were kind, gentle and professional, although I was in no mood to be cooperative. I was never outwardly obstructive. I simply stood on my dignity and was determined to let nobody get to know the real me. I was also perplexed by the fact that they studiously avoided the word 'blind'. They continually told us that we were visually impaired people—with the accent on people! I concluded that this was done so as to hide reality from the expectant.

By now my sight had disimproved even more than I had imagined when Professor Rosenthal explained it to me. Objects in close proximity didn't exist and my ability to recognize people had disappeared. There was a large, grey space of nothingness that increasingly filled itself with fear, alcohol and bad temper. Many times I wanted to cry for help but my need for self-sufficiency would not permit it.

Two days after my arrival at Dorton College I met Susan. Susan was in her early twenties, attractive and blind. She worked for the Royal London Society for the Blind, the owners of the establishment, and she helped to install and maintain programs on their computers. Her speciality was access technology. This was the hardware and software that allowed the sightless to gain access to the world of information technology.

'How did you lose your sight?' I asked her.

'When I was a child I was playing at school and another student hit me in the head with a model aeroplane. I lost my sight.' Susan's guide dog stirred in his basket.

'Are you angry?' I asked.

'Bloody right I am,' says she.

'But it was an accident,' says I.

'Oh, I'm not angry with the kid. I'm angry that nothing was done about it.'

'How do you mean?' I asked.

'There should have been some form of compensation or something.'

'You mean money?'

'I know it sounds awful, but yes.'

I knew what she meant. I was feeling the same thing. Why *should* this happen to me and the whole world not have to pay for it? 'So what do you do now?' I asked.

'I get on with things. It has advantages you know.'

'How?'

'Boyfriends all look really great. I can make them look like Steve McQueen, whatever he looks like.'

'He's gorgeous.' I described him from memory and then we laughed. 'Maybe this blindness isn't so bad after all,' I joked.

'It has other advantages too.'

'Tell me.'

'When you are less angry,' she replied. The story of Scheherazade sprang to mind.

Spencer loved three things—life, women and beer, and not necessarily in that order. 'When my bosses found out I couldn't see properly they fired me,' he told me one evening over a pint of bitter.

'I resigned before they found out,' I lied.

'Here's to them,' he laughed. 'Who cares.' He raised his beer in mock salute.

'What were you working at anyway?' I asked.

'I was a security guard.'

My pint went down the wrong way. 'A flaming security guard!' I exclaimed. Spencer chuckled. 'A flaming blind security guard!' I was astonished and I sounded it.

'It worked alright until I stopped the wrong person for shoplifting. Then I began walking into glass doors. Then I got the sack.' Spencer saw the whole thing as one big joke.

'What about you? What did you do?' he asked.

'I worked in the finance world,' I told him.

'Suppose you need to see to keep books,' he replied.

'Keep flaming books,' says I indignantly. 'I cooked the bastards.'

We slapped one another's backs and downed our pints. Spencer ordered two more pints and went silent for a couple of moments. 'Look mate,' he told me, 'blind equals unemployed. That's a fact of life so you had better get used to it. The way I see it, you have two options. Option one, work for do-good charities doing nothing jobs for small pay. Option two, learn the system, draw the old jam roll, and become the highest-trained monkey in the zoo.'

'Jam roll?' says I.

'Cockney rhyme for dole. You know, unemployment benefit for the posh amongst us.'

'It's got to be better than that,' I protested.

'Look at the facts, mate. How many blind people have you worked with?'

'None.'

'Exactly. Do you know anyone who has worked with a blind person?'

'No.'

'Winner all right,' he concluded.

We drank solidly for the rest of the evening. Spencer wanted to enjoy himself. I wanted to escape. Only Spencer succeeded.

Bang! You're Dead

After the pub closed we got sighted assistance back to the college. Spencer and I linked arms and sang the Mickey Mouse song all the way back, kicking our heels in the air at the appropriate times.

The next day I met Susan at the computer room. I told her about my chat with Spencer the previous evening. 'It's true for most people,' she confirmed. 'But it won't be for me. I'm going to study psychology and I'm flaming well going to practise as a child psychologist.'

'How many blind psychologists are there?'

'Don't know,' she replied, 'and I don't care. Where is it written that I can't be the first, except in my head?'

'Don't know,' says I. I didn't want to tell her about my three hundred failed applications.

'Do you know your problem?' she asked.

'No.'

'You're so far up your own backside the lights have gone out.'

'You looking for a slap in the puss or what?' says I.

'Look at all the talents you've been given. Look at the great life you've had up to now. Look at the inspiration you could be to others like me, like Spencer. But all you want to do is stick you nose in a glass and abdicate. That's your real disability—lack of balls not lack of sight.'

'Who asked you?' I retorted coldly and walked out.

Three days later Susan came to see me in my room. It was eleven in the morning and I had just opened a bottle of wine. 'Care for a glass?' I asked.

She ignored the offer. 'Sorry,' she began, 'I didn't mean to get angry at you the other day.'

'No probs. You said what you thought.'

'I didn't really.'

'Well then?'

'Well, yeah I was mad, but not at you. It's just … well, if a guy like you can't make it, what hope have the rest of us got?'

'What do you mean, like me?'

'Look at all your qualifications and life experience and you still can't get a job. So what do I do?'

'Study psychology and become the first blind psychologist in England,' I replied.

'What if I can't?'

'You can,' I reassured her.

'And if I don't, do I end up inside a bottle like you?' I had no answer for that and quite frankly I didn't care.

About a week later the head of the college, Brian Cooney, called me to his office. 'What do you really want to do with your life?' he asked me. Brian was a big chap with a broad, friendly Liverpool accent.

'I'd love to be a writer,' I told him. It was just one of many ideas I had been toying with and it sounded good.

'Good choice,' he chuckled. 'Writers, I mean the good ones, have to suffer a lot. It increases their circulation.' He laughed loudly. Brian was outgoing and built like a tank with a voice that was confident and full of enthusiasm. To this day I cannot tell you what he looks like, although I count him amongst one of my good friends. 'You hurt enough to do something about it yet, kid?' he asked.

'Huh?'

'Writers all have one thing in common. They write. Have you started?'

'I have a few ideas,' I told him. 'Anyway, how many blind writers do you know?'

'Lots. Writers, journalists, broadcasters, bankers, wasters. You name it.'

'All well paid?' I asked.

'Don't know,' he admitted 'But is that important?'

'It's a measure,' I replied.

'Of what?'

'Of success,' says I.

'Whose success?'

'Mine.'

'Is that what you want to write for? Money?'

'That's not fair,' I retaliated.

'So what is? You tell me.'

'Not being blind.'

'But you are.'

'Shit. You noticed, eh?

'It's my job.'

'Do you get paid a lot?'

'Quite a lot.'

'See,' I concluded.

'See what?'

'I'm blind,' I spat. 'I won't get paid a lot.'

'That might be so. It doesn't have to be. You probably won't be paid as much as you were before. But before, that was before. Wasn't it?'

'What d'ya mean?'

'When it comes time for you to draw your last breath, will you be flattered if all people can say about you is that once he made a lot of money, then he went blind. Then he drank booze.'

'I . . .'

'Look at yourself,' he told me, 'hung over and beaten. All that has changed in your life is your sight. You are still the same man. So go out and show them.'

'I can't,' I admitted. 'I'm afraid.'

I heard the words. I knew they related to me and I knew I had said them. But I couldn't recall ever having identified fear as something I felt. But as soon as I had said the words I felt relieved.

'Of course you are, son,' he confirmed. 'So would I be. But fear won't stop the sun rising in the morning, nor will the birds stop singing. It sure as hell won't have any effect on the stock market. But it's okay to be afraid. It's our job to help you through it. But *you* have to be there. *You* have to want to change.'

'I'll do my best,' I promised. That evening I slept soundly for the first time in months.

'What are you worth—love or money?' this big green serpent asked me.

'Love,' I shouted defiantly. And the serpent began to laugh. 'Love, love,' I cried even louder. The snake disappeared. Father Tim replaced the snake. He was a tall saintly man. But I recognized him as the Jesuit priest I had spoken to on a school retreat many years ago.

We were walking around a flower-encircled garden. I knew we were in Ireland from the crisp freshness of the air and the sound of a distant cuckoo. I noticed he was wearing no socks. 'Why do you not wear socks, Father?' I asked him as we began our walk around the garden.

'Humility, lad,' he replied.

'What's that, Father?' says I.

'It's a kind of courage,' says the sainted pastor.

'Courage, Father? Ya mean like Audie Murphy?'

'No lad. It's a kind of courage that takes away the fear of living.'

'Living, Father?' says I. 'Who's afraid of living?'

'Most of us are, lad, at some point in our lives.'

'Ah feck off, Father,' says I, 'you're having me on.'

'One of the great prizes of youth, lad, is that we think we are indestructible. We believe we can achieve anything we want—just because we want it. During this time we forget about Him.' He looked heavenward and then in the direction of a statue of the Blessed Virgin that stood amongst a clump of grass. It needed mowing. Thorns and briars clung to the lonely statue.

'And one day,' he continued, 'if we are lucky, we come to a crossroads. On the right is the gift of love. On the left is the gift of material things. There's nothing wrong with either. Both have their advantages. But most people turn left because they don't have the courage to choose love. You see, lad, it does take courage to choose the path of love and that courage is called humility.'

'So what you are telling me, Father,' says I incredulously, 'is that it takes more guts and determination to love someone than it does to make a lot of money.'

'That's what I'm saying, lad,' says he. 'And what's more, lad, the greatest courage of all is the ability to like yourself.'

'Ah now you're really feckin' kidding me, Father,' says I.

'No lad. I'm not kidding you.' He quickened his pace as we neared the gate and the pathway back to the retreat house. 'Tell you what,' says he as he opened the squeaking gate, 'each day I'll remember you in my prayers and ask that, if it's God's will, you will choose the right path.'

'Thank you, Father,' says I.

When I woke up the next morning I remembered the dream vividly and wondered if it had really happened. But I was certain it hadn't.

I spent the remainder of my time at Dorton learning how to use computers with speech packages so that I didn't need to be able to read the screen. I discovered that letters scanned into the computer could be read back to me. I even learned how to walk safely with a white cane and got over the embarrassment of people looking at me and wanting to help me cross the road even when I didn't want to.

I left Dorton determined to continue trying and I didn't know where the idea of becoming a writer came from. I think I made it up on the spot just to impress. But the more I thought about it, the better the idea became. I even researched a few colleges that offered courses in creative writing and I resolved to attend one of them.

As I was leaving Dorton the place felt full of the hope and courage of a Tchaikovsky symphony. It had lost its cold feeling, which I now realized had nothing to do with the buildings. It had everything to do with my feelings of inadequacy.

Through professionalism and real love this place had achieved for me what I couldn't achieve for myself—an acceptance that things are today exactly as they are supposed to be. I was blind and this condition would be part of me until the day I died.

I spent the next year learning how to write. The University of Manchester accepted me on a postgraduate degree course and the year was one of the most amazing experiences I have ever had. My eyes were opened to the beauty of literature and the arts.

And as the year drew to a close and we left to prepare our novels for submission, I felt so privileged to have been given the opportunity to have studied under two such eminent men as Dr Richard Francis and Michael Schmidt. They lit within me a passion to express myself in words that will remain alight until I die.

The year unlocked a creativity I never knew I possessed and it meant more to me than money. So now I was able to relate to the chat I had with Brian Cooney two years previously. Money was not a measure of success. Although I knew I wanted to write so badly I could burst, I still had not totally beaten the old me. I still drank and I still hated being blind and I still hated the world for seeing me as a blind person. I was only halfway home but the journey towards total acceptance had begun.

Chapter Eight

London

August 1996

I had given up all hope of getting a job and I was busy perfecting a novel I was working on when I received a letter from the Employment Service inviting me to visit Wendy Craddock. I knew it wouldn't be of much use but failure to respond to their commands would mean the end of my benefits.

Wendy was as bubbly and as full of confidence as ever. 'I've been thinking about you,' she told me.

'Not coming between you and your sleep I hope,' says I. Wendy laughed. 'I've been working on a novel,' I told her. She seemed genuinely impressed, but I was certain she had heard the story of the two novelists in the pub.

One novelist says to the other, 'What are you at, dear chap?'

'I'm writing a novel,' says the other.

'That's odd,' the first one replies, 'neither am I.'

But then again, she may not have heard of it and was just impressed that a blind man could write or would want to.

'I've met a chap I would like you to meet,' she continued. 'His name is Andy Taylor. He's the best person I know at getting visually impaired people into work and he's totally blind.'

I tried to look impressed but I felt myself wondering what Wendy looked like and why in hell I should want to raise my hopes about even getting a job just when I had become comfortable about my unemployability. 'Love to meet him,' I lied.

'How are you, Tommy boy,' Andy said as he groped for my hand. His handshake was firm and confident, his palms a little moist. Liver trouble, I decided.

'Not too bad,' says I.

'I don't know what Wendy told you about me, but I'm the best.'

'So am I,' I responded. Andy chuckled, I didn't.

'Right,' he continued, 'so you want a job. Do you have a curriculum vitae?'

'Yes.' I handed him the document that had been prepared by the consultant a couple of years earlier. He handed it to his assistant, Tom, who sat behind a portable partition.

The office was small and cluttered with the paraphernalia that helped visually impaired people read the printed word or operate computers. Andy seemed friendly but I didn't get a feeling that I was going to find a job through this source.

Still Andy seemed nice enough to at least give it a go. Tom announced that the document was fine and even added it was one of the best he had seen. 'Can't be too careful,' says Andy. 'Most of the people we get here don't know how to put a CV together.'

'Really,' says I. 'What type of jobs do you find for people?'

'Most of our clients are visually impaired. It's harder than buggery to find a job for a blind man. Camels and eyes of needles spring to mind, actually. We get all sorts of jobs. I got a job for a chap last week with the Metropolitan Police.'

'So what ...?'

'About you,' he interrupted. 'I never give up. That's why things work for me. I get things done through persistence and that's what you are going to need. Persistence.'

'I'll do my best,' says I and then I wondered if he heard the smirk in my voice. If he did, he didn't let on.

'Let me give you some facts,' he began. 'Seventy-five percent of visually impaired people have no job—zippo. They go into the benefit system from school and never get out of it. You are lucky. You had the chance to work and gain experience but it's unlikely that you will regain your former glory. Unlikely, I say, but not impossible. That's up to you.'

'Seventy-five percent!' says I.

'Eighty-five if you happen to be a visually impaired woman.'

'Why?' I didn't disguise my amazement.

' 'Cos nobody gives a damn. We are too much bother in a fast-moving society. So you'll probably have to work in the charitable sector or if you're really lucky you might land a government job.'

'But I know nothing about charities and all that.'

He laughed. 'Don't worry. Don't let ignorance stop you. It doesn't stop anyone else. Just remember, you have a lot to offer.'

'So what next?'

'Leave everything to me. I'll scan for jobs for you, you apply and eventually I'll chalk you up as another success!'

A week later I contacted Andy at his office near Euston in North London. 'Hi, it's Tom,' says I.

'Tommy, my boy, how the hell are you?'

'Fine.'

'What can I do for ya, lad?'

Stop being so bloody happy, I thought.

'I was thinking about what you said,' I told him, 'and I think it's a bloody disgrace that so many blind people can't get jobs.'

'History, me boy,' he replied. 'History.'

'But it must change,' I insisted.

'It will. If people like you talk openly about it for long enough. Feel up to the job?'

I told Andy how I felt at being unemployable, the unanswered letters of application, my despair and low self-worth. The whole monologue took over an hour. He barely interrupted me except to agree.

'Sounds like you want to do something about it,' he concluded.

'Yes,' says I, and for the first time since I left that hospital in Baltimore I felt as if I had a purpose in life.

'Good. I can help, but only if you want to help yourself.'

'I think I do,' I told him.

'So let's get to it, Tommy boy.'

We hung up with Andy promising to get in touch 'real soon'. In the meantime I was to remember that the greatest help I could be to the cause of unemployment amongst the blind was to get a job myself.

About two weeks passed and I hadn't heard from Andy. I thought he had forgotten about me. I decided to give him another day and then I would contact him.

The phone rang. It was Andy. 'Tommy, me boy, 'tis I,' he announced. We exchanged pleasantries. 'Remember we spoke about the unemployment rate amongst visually impaired people?'

'I can't think of much else,' I replied.

'A group of charities are putting together a bit of a bash-up at the House of Commons. Think you would be able to say a few words?'

Damn.

'Told ya, Tommy. You either want to help or you don't.'

'I want to help,' I confirmed.

Andy explained that a number of leading charities for the blind had come together under the banner of an organisation called Opsis, and they wanted to highlight the fact that the unemployment rate amongst people like me was unacceptably high. 'More like a bloody disgrace,' Andy commented. He told me that they were mounting a national campaign that included press, radio and television and that the meeting at the House of Commons would be chaired by a leading politician, a woman who cared deeply about human rights.

'Seems high-powered,' says I.

'Only the best,' Andy replied, 'and about bloody time too.' He went on to explain that a number of charities including Action for Blind People, Guide Dogs, the Royal National Institute for the Blind and my old friends from Dorton (the Royal London Society for the Blind) would be involved and that, besides me, the speakers would include the chief executive of Lambeth Borough Council, a senior manager from Thames Water, and the BBC correspondent Peter White, who covers disability issues.

'You need to tell them what you have done to get a job,' he told me. 'Tell them, Tommy boy, how the system has dicked you around. Us blind folk need someone like you who can talk, just to let people know how unfair the bloody world is to us.'

'That's what everyone with difficulty says,' I told him.

Pause. 'So you think you can live life on your own, Tommy boy. You think you have nothing to offer anyone else just because you find yourself with eyes that are not too clever. You know what you are? A sad bastard. That's what.'

'Steady on,' I told him.

'Sorry,' he replied. 'I just get so mad thinking about the fact that people like you can't get a decent job just because you can't see. I deal with it every day—the human remains I call them.'

'What I meant was that single-interest groups always seem to come across as cranks. That's all.'

'So you need to use the power of persuasion to let them know that we genuinely need help.'

'I'll do my best,' I agreed.

'And that will be good enough. The sight of a blind man doing his best always brings tears to their eyes.' We laughed but we really meant to be angry.

By the time it came to my turn to speak, all my nervousness had disappeared. The invited audience, most of whom were chosen from the converted, listened with great interest as I told my story and catalogued the effects unemployment had on me and four hundred thousand others like me. My words confirmed their worst suspicions—blind people found it more difficult to gain employment than any other form of disability. Indeed it was three times more difficult for a visually impaired person to get a job than a deaf person and twice as hard as someone with a learning difficulty.

Yet each of the speakers, visually impaired and employed alike, seemed to echo the valid frustrations of people like me. Those who were in a position to employ promised to do better in the future. After all, blind people were people too!

All went well in a mantric sort of way. Everyone was satisfied that the problem existed. This gave the converted new energy to continue the fight. It also gave the employers a fresher slogan with which to protest their political correctness. The politicians had satisfied their duty to listen and the unemployment rate amongst the blind would continue to rise. This would give everyone another opportunity to gather in a couple of years time and repeat the process.

I sat behind the velvet-covered tables and looked across an unseeable ocean of heads. I wondered who amongst them cared enough for the cause—not on an intellectual level but deep down in a belly that burned with a fire sort of way. I realized that those would be few in number and even fewer would possess the skill and connections necessary to cause a fundamental shift in the attitudes of British society to the needs of the disadvantaged.

The chairman called on me to sum up what I really felt. This was not part of the agenda. I began to shake. The assembled quietened and awaited my newest words of affirmation. All I could think of was a joke someone had told me, so I decided to tell it. 'Madam Chairman,' says I, 'what visually impaired people need more than anything else is a level playing field; a chance to prove that they can do as well as everyone else. For a person such as myself it is indeed a very humbling experience to stand here where Daniel O'Connell once pleaded for home rule for my country of birth. He asked the Great British nation for a chance to be treated honourably and appealed to their generosity of spirit. Today I find myself in a similar, though less historic, position!'

I paused for a moment and scrambled for the words that might ignite a new perspective in the converted; cause them to rise up and express the fury I felt at being made to feel less than useful by a society that publicly embraced the principles of equality of opportunity. But none came. 'Madam Chairman,' I continued, 'I would like to tell you a little joke.' I could feel her surprise, and the tension of the converted rose as they began to feel that maybe, just maybe, this blind man whom they had entrusted with the responsibility of delivering their message, was now about to say something that would embarrass them.

'A blind man goes up to Arnold Palmer and says, "Arnold, I bet you ten quid I could beat you in a game of golf." "But I'm a professional," Arnold protests. "I know that," the blind man responds, "but I'll still bet you ten quid." Palmer becomes desperate. "But you're blind," he says, a little embarrassed at referring to the man's obvious disability. "I know that better than most," the blind man replies confidently, "but I still bet you ten quid." "Okay," says Palmer, "when do you want to play?" The blind man pauses and strokes his chin thoughtfully before replying, "Any night you're free!" '

The audience laughed. To this day I'm not sure if it was because they thought the joke was funny or from sheer relief. Then the laughter subsided and I began to speak again. 'All the blind man felt he needed, my friends, was a level playing field.' I turned in the direction of the famous politician in the chair. 'Madam Chairman,' says I, 'only you can provide it.'

What followed was a week of press, radio and television interviews. All were conducted in the best of taste yet nobody seemed as angry as I. But I realized that anger was no weapon against injustice.

A month later the phone rang. It was Andy. 'Hiya, Tommy boy.'

'Good.'

'Good news, Tommy boy. You have an interview for a job.'

Silence.

'Yes, Tommy boy, it's an East London borough. The job's made for you.' He told me that the job was acting as a business advisor to local small businesses in the East End of London. 'You could do it blindfold,' he chuckled.

About a week later I went for a psychometric test and initial interview. The local authority could not have been more helpful. They provided the magnification equipment I needed to read the test papers and even helped with the ticking of the boxes on the form for the psychometric test. The interview gave no ground to my disability. They wanted to know everything I had done. I can safely say it was one of the most in-depth interviews I have ever attended.

When I got home I rang Andy. 'They want me back for a second interview,' I told him.

'Knew it. You've got the qualifications. They want the best man for the job and they don't worry about your disability so long as you can do the job.'

'I suppose,' I conceded.

'Look, Tommy boy, once you get your foot inside the door you will shoot up the ladder.'

'If I see it,' I joked.

'Want to know something else, Tommy boy?'

'What?' says I.

'I have another job that's just made for you.'

'Tell me about it,' says I.

'It's with Action for Blind People. They're looking for someone to help blind geezers get a job. Interested?'

'Okay. I'll give it a twirl. What do I do now?'

'Just ring this number. They'll send you a form. Fill it in and send it back.'

'But I've never worked in employment,' says I.

'Neither did I, once.'

I rang the charity and the operator put me through to an answering machine. I left my details and the name of the job that interested me.

About a week later a large brown envelope arrived with a covering letter stating that they were delighted I had applied for the post of factory general manager and that they had enclosed a job description, person specification, application form and a copy of their equal opportunities policy.

I rang Andy. 'They sent me the wrong job,' says I.

'Nothing in this world ever happens by accident,' he tells me.

'Bullshit,' says I.

'Contempt prior to investigation,' he retorts. 'Just read the documents, see if you like the job and go for it.'

Two days later I dropped my completed application form in the post, happy in the knowledge that I would get an interview anyway. Their equal opportunities policy almost guaranteed one because I was disabled. And I had more than enough qualifications to do the job.

Sure enough, a week later I was called for an interview at their Verney Road headquarters. The interview was tough and searching and left no stone unturned as to my previous experience and qualifications. 'Have you any questions?' Tony Giller asked. Tony was a smallish man with a lively, kind voice that brimmed with sincerity.

'You never asked me about my blindness,' says I.

'It doesn't affect your ability to do the job,' he replied.

'Well ... ' I hesitated.

Tony explained that I needed to have confidence in myself and that the charity would support me in every way possible. 'After all,' he concluded, 'it would seem hypocritical to us if we were asking employers to hire blind people when we close the door on them ourselves just because of a little difficulty.'

'True,' I replied.

Now I really wanted this job. Not for the money but because I could get a chance to prove to myself that I could do it. Tony Giller seemed confident in my ability and that helped me a lot. 'Would you like to see the factory?' he asked. I agreed and he took me though a labyrinth of corridors to a factory that was totally staffed by blind people.

'Everyone here is blind,' he boasted over the noise of the machinery. 'We hire a few sighted people and their job is to support those who cannot see, whenever that is necessary.' I was impressed and said so. 'This factory operates at break-even, or that's the theory,' he laughed.

'If I got the job what would you expect me to do?'

'Secure the long-term viability of the unit and enrich the lives of those working here. Simple?' I hesitated. Nobody had ever asked me to enrich lives before. Normally it was profit, or the need to increase productivity or cash flow.

One of the workers approached us, oblivious to our existence. 'Hiya Larry,' Tony said. 'It's Tony Giller.'

Larry's face beamed. 'Hi, Tony.'

'I have a chap here with me. His name is Tom Pey and he is hoping to be the next general manager of the factory.'

'Not blind then?' Larry retorted.

'As a matter of fact I am,' I told him.

'Good,' he replied, 'we need one of our own here. Know what I mean?'

'No,' says I.

'It's great here,' he replied, 'don't get me wrong. But we need someone with a bit of education who can explain what we mean—from our point of view. The professionals do their best but they don't understand. Do you find that, Tom, you know? Who can tell you what's inside your head except someone who has walked in your shoes?'

'I think I know what you mean,' I lied.

'How much can you see?' he asked.

His directness threw me. 'A little. Peripheral.'

'A little is great. Me, I'm total. Born that way.'

'I'm sorry.'

'Don't be. They say it's easier. You know, you never miss what you never had.'

'And do you?'

'Don't know. I get pissed off sometimes because I can't see but most of the time it's okay.'

'What do you think needs to happen here in the factory?' I asked.

'More pay, less hours and more fag breaks,' he replied without hesitation.

I laughed. Nothing changes. Every factory worker in the world would want the same thing.

That night I began thinking about the interview, cursing the answers I had given that could have been better. I really wanted this job.

Why?

I don't know. All I know is that it felt right for me. It felt clean and simple inside and I liked that feeling. I felt as if I could like myself doing this job and that was something I had never even thought about before.

It took a week, a second interview and lots of praying. But I got the job!

The Verney Road factory of Action for Blind People manufactured PVC- and leather-covered binders for the quality end of the stationery market.

I started on the fourth of April and immediately went into action. In any review of a business (and I saw the factory primarily as a business) one needs to establish the current position. This took a couple of weeks. I ploughed through past statistics and although these tended to be scanty, and in most cases did not measure the right things, I was able to establish that sales volumes and prices had been static for three years and cost increase pressures were kept under control by cutting down on maintenance, the purchase of new machinery and marketing costs. A quick scan around the stationery industry, and specifically other PVC binder manufacturers, showed that the marketplace was price sensitive and that shop prices were being forced down by cheap imports from the Far East.

The productivity in the factory was around twenty percent of open industry standards, so the factory was only surviving because a few local authorities were paying the charity to provide sheltered workshop facilities for the blind people of their boroughs.

It was easy to establish output levels. All you had to do was to stand beside a machine and listen to its slow, laborious banging as it completed a cycle of operation. By reading the manuals one could establish the full capacity of the machines and it was a safe bet that open industry would work its machinery to around seventy-five percent of capacity.

I rang someone I knew at the Royal National Institute for the Blind and asked them for a potted history of sheltered workshops. They started in Victorian times and were originally set up as an alternative to sending a blind person to the insane asylum. The blind person was shown how to make baskets and was taught the Bible. Conditions were poor but a lot better than the alternative.

In the 1920s Action for Blind People became the first workshop provider in the world to allow blind men to operate powered machinery. This was an earth-shattering development. Up until then blind people were credited with imbecilic intelligence and qualities. That was because a lot of them rocked when they sat down, so people mixed this up with psychotic behaviour. But this rocking motion is caused by a lack of human contact.

Mothers who couldn't manage their blind children placed them in institutions. They were never cuddled or rocked. So they began rocking back and forth themselves. The public misinterpreted the symptoms. Near to the end of the 1920s, Action for Blind People allowed women the same privileges as men. They too could operate powered machinery. In this way the charity could claim to be the first equal opportunities employer in the world. Their example spread and soon most workshops were allowing blind people to use powered machinery, and they began to produce goods that had a commercial value. They began competing with those made by sighted folk.

And then came the Second World War. Blind people joined in the war effort and used their newly acquired skills to produce parts for Spitfires, shell casings and all the other trappings needed at the time. This led to a post-war statement in the House of Commons to the effect that blind people were entitled to 'meaningful' work. The structure of the workshops changed as they strove to increase productivity and reduce reliance on government support.

'And did it work?' says I.

'No, the management of the workshops were more concerned with helping blind people, in inverted commas, than facilitating them to help themselves. This is where they are today. The sheltered workshops have become a place of institutionalized labour. But the good thing is that the New Labour government are hot to trot on human rights, equality and all that. I wouldn't be surprised if they abolished sheltered employment as a concept.'

'But they would still need to replace it with something else—until employers begin to see the value of visually impaired employees and begin employing them,' says I.

'Huh,' says she and she hangs up.

Our strengths were that our productivity was so low it couldn't get any worse, we produced an extremely high-quality product and our major customer, Dudley Stationery, was extremely loyal. Our threat was the possible government attitude to sheltered employment. One day I told all the employees how I was going to help turn the factory around. 'It's simple,' says I, 'all we need to do is sell more binders.'

'He wants us to work harder,' they murmured.

'We thought you were one of us,' someone complained.

I was flabbergasted. Couldn't they see that increased sales

meant that their jobs were safer and their long-term future secure. I put this to them.

'If you want more sales, you need to get more workers,' they told me.

'But your productivity is less than twenty percent of open industry.'

'Of course it is,' they replied, 'we're blind.'

'That's all we are,' I protested. 'We are only blind. And think of the four hundred thousand of us out there who don't have a job. What about them? How can we ask employers to hire them if all they can expect is twenty percent productivity?'

Silence.

'I'm not saying you need to work harder,' I continued. 'Yes, you will. But not seventy-five percent harder. We do, however, need to work smarter. Just think of the jobs you are doing. Can we improve the way you do the job?'

'Yeah. Get your Irish friends to blow the place up,' someone shouted.

'No can do,' I replied. 'Come on,' I urged, 'just think of the little things you have always asked for and were refused in the past.'

'It's okay for you to talk, boss,' someone said, 'but there's no money whenever we do ask.'

'Just give me a chance,' I asked. 'I know we can do things differently.'

They did and matters did improve. Within a year sales were up thirty-five percent, even though we had to reduce our prices by fifteen percent to meet competition. Factory productivity soared and for the first time in my life, I saw people's enthusiasm for the greater good overcome huge obstacles. These people were not bothered by the business need. They saw themselves as blind people, led by a blind man, who could help others in a similar predicament to get a job. All they had to do was to show the world that they could do it. Management now had to listen to them. And we did.

I had arrived at Action for Blind People believing I was a gifted manager who could bring commercial realism to bear on a quasi-commercial venture. One year later I learned that a true leader—one who is blessed with a modicum of humility—can facilitate the growth of something great. These people only needed someone to allow them to trust themselves. Once this was achieved, and it didn't happen overnight, they were spurred on by the need to prove to themselves that they were as good as anyone else. They complained when production was delayed or when an order was delivered late. They took on responsibility for health and safety. They became a team of talented people.

And me? I became a facilitator; an intermediary between enthusiasm and what was possible. We weathered storms over the next six months, laughed a lot and argued a little. But it worked.

After twenty months in the job I saw an advertisement for operations director at the Guide Dogs for the Blind Association and I applied for it.

I gained my first impressions of Guide Dogs about four years earlier when I applied to be trained with a dog and I was accepted. 'I know you could probably survive without a guide dog right now,' Professor Rosenthal told me. 'But your vision will deteriorate for the next five years or so and then it will stabilize.' I was frightened by the prospect of handing my life over to a dog, no matter how well trained it might be. Furthermore, I was just getting used to the idea of walking with a white cane.

Walking with a white cane was a very public admission for me that I was a blind man. It was also an invitation for well-meaning folk to grab your arm as you were about to board a train in the belief that somehow you did not possess the ability to get around on your own. I knew these people only wanted to help but I wished they would ask my permission first. I know it sounds petty but nobody would rush up to a sighted person, grab their arm and say, 'Come on, dear. I'll look after you'—only if they wanted their lights punched out.

But they did it to me and I had to bear this intrusion on my privacy. Having a dog, I knew, would make matters ten times worse. 'The number of times I was standing in a railway station,' Susan told me, 'and people rush up to you and say, "Hello, beautiful." They actually mean the dog.' I laughed. 'It sounds funny in the telling,' she complained. 'But then they expect you to stand there and talk to them when all you want to do is piss off home.'

It was June and my Dad died of a stroke about three weeks earlier. I was not yet at the point where I felt the loss of him. I kept all feelings well at bay with copious amounts of wine.

Mimi dropped me off at the Wokingham Centre, which was situated about thirty miles south-west of London. It was a warm day and I was introduced to seven other blind people but only one other was like me—being trained with their first dog. The routines of the day were explained to us and we were told we would have to remain at the centre for three weeks.

'I love it here,' Janet told me. Janet was a rather large, good-humoured woman from South-east London.

'Why?' says I.

'The grub's bloody marvellous.'

'This is my third,' a chirpy little man from Crawley told me. His name was Alan. He appeared to be in his late fifties.

Alan, Janet and I became good friends and we called ourselves the Flowerpot Men. We christened Janet 'Little Weed' and every time we called her name she would say 'Balub alub aluba'. That was how boring the days were between the training sessions!

On the third day I was introduced to my guide dog. His name was Martin. Coincidentally that was also my middle name, and my Dad had performed with a chap who sang and played guitar, and his name was also Martin. So I would have no trouble remembering the name!

Martin was simply gorgeous. He was a yellow Labrador and was so, so gentle yet extremely gregarious. I loved him instantly. But then I have always loved dogs since I was a little lad in knee-length trousers. I think Martin was a little hesitant about me at first. But I just knew that we would get on together.

The training regime was strict, bordering on the militaristic at times. The instructor told me what to do and I struggled with the decision as to whether I would do what I was told or what I thought was best. 'Don't argue with them,' Little Weed told me one day as we sat in the training van waiting for our turn to walk with our dog.

'Why not?' says I.

'They'll send you home without a dog,' says she.

'They can and they will,' Alan warned.

That was enough for me. No more lip. I would do exactly

as I was told. The instructions came thick and fast, and for the first time in my life I began to suffer from a mixture of total confusion and mild anxiety. 'There's a lot going on in your life,' Little Weed said one night as we ate sandwiches in the students' lounge. 'What with yer Dad dyin' and all.'

'I know,' says I.

'The problem is,' says Alan, 'this is no place to get counselling. Here ya do what you're told and leave yer problems outside.' I tried to do this but I had a feeling that I was being judged for who I was and not what I could become. I wanted to tell these people how desperately horrible it was to be in the room when my Dad died and not be able to see his face. Ma told me he looked very peaceful but I just needed to see this for myself.

'Keep yerself to yerself,' Little Weed warned and I did.

Despite being told that I was almost dismissed from class because of my inability to work with the dog, I eventually qualified and became a fully certified guide dog owner. But the best comment stuck with me: 'I'm sure it was well earned.'

The copious amounts of wine and beer I consumed dulled my capabilities. And my passion for dogs, Labradors in particular, and the fact that I had trained many dogs as gundogs when I lived in Ireland had not stood me in good stead at Wokingham. To me, my blindness had simply robbed me of yet another talent. But a year later I was to add the Wokingham experience to many others and I quit drinking for good.

I only had my dog about a month when we ventured into London together. We took the train from Bromley to Victoria and we walked around the city until I could do no more.

It was warm and I had forgotten to bring money and I was as thirsty as hell. I got Martin a bowl of water in a nearby cafe and the owner stood there talking to the dog as he lapped up the cool liquid. 'Here, son,' says he. 'Have a Coke.' He handed me a cool can of cola and I could have kissed him, only I wasn't sure what he looked like.

I decided to hold on to the can of Coke until I was seated on the train, because I needed my two hands to control and direct the dog. About fifteen minutes later I was sitting on the train back to Bromley. I pulled the ring on my can of Coke and took a long luxurious sip.

'Your dog is lovely,' an old lady's voice told me. She was sitting opposite.

'Thank you,' says I and I took another swig of my coke.

The old lady appeared to be rummaging in her handbag. 'You collecting for Guide Dogs?' she asks.

'No,' says I.

'Here,' says she and she dropped a coin into my can of coke.

I wanted to strangle her but instead I thanked her for her generosity.

'We want to be a client-focused organization,' David Ellis told me at the interview. David was the director of services for the association and was responsible for delivering all of the services to clients.

'I'm your man,' says I. 'Who better to help with client focus than a client?' David believed me and I got the job. Now I help to ensure that all of our clients are recognized for who they could be and how we can help bridge any gap that might exist.

Today the Guide Dogs for the Blind Association delivers a professional service to clients. We see our mission in life as one of ensuring that all visually impaired people should be able to get around safely whether with a dog or a white cane. I am delighted to be part of this forward-thinking team and to have the opportunity of putting client concerns to our professionals so that together we can deliver the world-class service for which we became renowned.

Chapter Nine

It was a Friday like any other Friday. The Underground was hot and clammy as hassled commuters competed for the honour of being first to start the weekend. Martin and I navigated our way through the throng, grateful for the space they made for us as overly hot commuters scrunched closer together to allow us to board the Tube to Victoria.

'Isn't he gorgeous.' It was a woman's voice. It sounded throaty and attractive.

'Why thank you, miss,' says I. We both laughed and she patted the dog to clarify what she meant.

Most people looked forward to Friday. For me, however, probably a hangover from my period of perceived unemployability, it was almost as if, once I had stopped working for a period, my employers would wake up to the fact that they had employed a blind man. I knew this was both untrue and unreasonable, that I had earned the weekend break, but I was a man driven by continuous insecurity. By Sunday that feeling would have disappeared as Monday and a full workload loomed. It took nearly two years for me to really believe that I had a full and valid contribution to make and that I was only hired because of my worth.

I got off the train at Bromley South and made my way to the ticket barrier. The ticket inspector knew me and called me to the opened security gate.

'How is that dog of yours treating you today?' he asked.

'Ask him yourself,' I replied. This was our code for my permission for him to stroke the dog.

'You're a great boy,' he tells Martin as he tickles him under the chin. Martin's tail wags with pleasure.

I make my way towards the exit but turn right before reaching it. This was where I had arranged to meet Andy.

'I'll see you at six,' he told me on the phone, 'I've got someone who wants to meet you.'

'Where and when?' I ask.

'Six o'clock. Bromley South. On the right-hand side of the exit.'

'Inside or outside?' It pays to be precise when you can't see.

'Inside.'

I pressed my watch. It told me it was 6.05. Andy hadn't arrived yet. I felt a little annoyed even though a five-minute delay wasn't unreasonable.

At fifteen minutes past six, Andy still hadn't arrived and I began to wonder if I had heard his instructions incorrectly.

I tried outside the exit on the right-hand side but he wasn't there either. On the way in Martin's tail wagged. He had recognized somebody. Maybe it was Andy.

'Find Andy,' I told him. Even though he hadn't been shown how to recognize Andy, it was worth a try. He pulled me to the right as we came back through the exit and stopped.

'Andy?' says I.

'Tommy, me boy,' says Andy, 'Where the hell were ya?'

'Over there,' says I. 'Right of the ticket barrier at the exit like you said.'

'No,' he insisted. 'I meant right of the exit as you come in. I got a lift to the station. Sorry, I thought you knew.'

We both laughed at our stupidity. It never crossed our minds to mourn our inabilities. After all, the problem was caused by our imprecise communications.

'Who's this person?' I asked.

'A young girl called Yvonne. Twenty-three years old. Diabetes. One day she could see just fine. The next day— nothing.'

'Rotten luck. She got no time to adjust.'

'Not good, Tommy boy. She is in a bit of a mess. She was a secretary up the City. She's totally confused about what she should do.'

Andy had arranged for me to meet Yvonne in a cafe across the road from the station.

'She's over there now with her father. I won't join you. She wants to speak to someone alone. Her father will leave you alone and you can call me on the mobile when you are finished. I'll talk to him in the meantime. He's as confused as she is, poor devil.'

I was taken across the road by one of the many helpful cabbies that park outside Bromley South station and Yvonne's father recognized me immediately and guided me to the table.

Yvonne Corey was small, slightly overweight and had a damp, limp handshake. She told me she was twenty-three and had been diagnosed with diabetes seven years previously.

'They told me it would affect my sight,' she continued, 'but they never used the word "blind".'

'They never do until the end,' I agreed.

'They didn't get time with me. Exactly four weeks and two days ago I got dressed for work as usual. It was a Wednesday morning. I liked Wednesdays the best because my boss always goes to a management meeting on Wednesday mornings and he doesn't get into his office until the afternoon. Anyway, I caught the train, had lunch with a friend, and finished my day's work. I was going to meet Dave, my boyfriend, that night. On the way home I began to feel a little unwell so I cancelled our date.'

'Did you notice anything about your sight?' I asked.

'No. Just a blinding headache.' She chuckled at the irony.

'Next morning,' she continued, 'I woke up. I knew I had opened my eyes but I couldn't see. I rubbed my eyes—but nothing. I began to scream but I live alone and nobody came. I fumbled for the phone and dialled 999. Eventually an ambulance came and brought me to hospital.'

'Do you still live alone? What about your boyfriend?'

'Ex-boyfriend,' she replied.

'Oh.'

'He freaked out. You'd think it happened to him.'

'Andy told me you had some questions.'

'I couldn't think of any when the specialist asked me. I feel so stupid now,' she admitted.

'Me too. I still feel stupid. I think it is a reaction to shock. It seems as if we have too much to deal with all at once to think of any real difficulties.'

'I suppose,' she agreed.

'I didn't want to admit to my sight loss,' I told her. 'Mine is not total. I have about five percent vision remaining.'

'What I wouldn't give just to see daylight again,' she replied.

'It must be awful,' I agreed.

Yvonne then began to tell me the story of her life, right from the beginning when she was a little child in Blackpool. It seemed to me that her frightened brain wanted to share its stored up memories lest they be lost forever. About an hour had elapsed when her stories finally dried up.

'Aren't you afraid?' she asked me. Her voice was quivering. I formed the impression that she had folded her arms in a type of self-hug.

'Scared shitless some of the time,' I admitted, 'but it gets easier. Aunt Lil told me once that you could get used to anything except hanging.'

'Aunt Lil?'

'She went blind too.'

'Oh.'

'All I can do is tell you what it was like for me,' I began. 'Take what you want from my experience and discard the rest. Okay?'

'Okay,' she agreed.

I then told her about my reaction to my sight loss. 'I behaved like a frightened child. I denied it was happening and drank like a fish to block out reality. But reality has a way of catching up with you only that in my case it really bit me in the ass.'

She laughed.

'I always thought of myself as a person of courage,' I continued. 'I thought God was generous to me when he was doling out guts. But I was wrong. I had mixed up bravado and real courage.'

'What's the difference?' she asked.

'Bravado is about the outward expression of bravery. You know, loud talking, big words. Intimidating others. But courage is about having the humility to accept reality as it really is—not how we might want it to be.'

'Why humility?' she asked.

'Because when you work in an important job like you or I, you begin to feel as if you ought to be in control of your surroundings. You tell people what to do, make important decisions that affect the lives of others without much thought as to the consequences. I know I talked fast and only listened when I had to.'

'And now?'

'Today I can honestly say that the only question I ask is, How can I help? I like being a part of things today. It's not necessary to be in control.'

'I'd hate to turn out like that,' she interrupted. 'It seems like you have thrown in the towel.'

'I suppose you are right. I have heard it described as surrendering to win.'

'Sounds clichéd.'

'It works for me. Oh, I argue like hell when I disagree with something but I don't throw my rattle out of the pram when the decision doesn't go my way. I suppose, I try to respect the opinions of others as much as I can but sometimes the little child in me comes out to play and I become over opinionated.'

'But that's all about you,' she complained. 'I'm fucking blind. How do I deal with that?'

I told her about white cane training and the notion of working with a guide dog like Martin. That is what we call mobility training and Guide Dogs can train you better than most.'

'A bleeding white cane. Now I'll really look like a blindee.'

'No offence,' I replied, 'but that is what you are.'

'I know,' she admitted. 'But I don't want to be. I really, really don't want to be blind.'

'Me neither,' I agreed. 'But just remember it's not always what happens to us that matters. It's how we deal with our circumstances that makes us into better people.'

I met Yvonne on a number of occasions after that and today she is a guide dog owner like me. She has also had a promotion in her job, which all goes to prove that, given half a chance, blind folk can do a worthwhile job.

Chapter Ten

Tom Pey
2001

I do not want to give you the impression that having come out from behind my shroud, I now tackle life with the ferocity of a religious convert. Far from it. Today I try to take the time that allows me to value other people. I learned the importance of this from Wendy Craddock, Andy Taylor and my friend Brian Cooney. If they had not taken the time to see the real me and to help me begin to care about myself, I would still be trapped in that mire of self-pity that almost sucked me under.

I have been given the chance to help others and each day I do this with the care I have learned from others. At this point I need to make a confession. It isn't simply I who tries to make a difference today. It is Martin and I who, together, make up a team that is willing to go the distance for another blind person.

Martin is a wonderful dog. His outgoing, gentle and caring personality remains unflapped when I go into a tizz. He leaves his lead under my office desk, stretches himself and sits at my feet inviting a reassuring pat on the head. Then I tell him how unfair the world is to blind people and how the statistics on unemployment amongst visually impaired people continue to disimprove despite my best efforts.

'What can I do, Martin?' says I. He yawns and nestles his head on my lap. 'I know Rome wasn't built in a day,' I tell him as I scratch behind his ear. He nestles a little closer. 'Perhaps you're right,' I continue. 'Maybe I need to talk to more people and little by little things will change.' He decides to go back to his bed. 'Don't run away like that,' I complain, 'just when our little chat is getting interesting.' He decides to ignore me and curls up on his fleece-lined blanket.

'I've even gotten a better idea,' says I. 'I'll write it down and maybe somebody who reads about the plight of young blind people will begin to get angry enough to do something. Or maybe one of the readers will be an employer and they will give a blind person a start in life. It doesn't have to be the biggest job in the world although that would be alright too.' I can hear Martin think: How will you know if it works? 'Maybe they will write to me or to Action for Blind People or to the Royal National Institute for the Blind. It's not important what they do except to give a blind person a start.'

'Better still,' Martin would say if he could talk (sometimes I think he can) 'why don't they ring the job centre and tell them they would like to hire a blind person. If every employer in England hired only one blind person each, there wouldn't be enough blind people to go around.'

'Good idea,' says I and I leave my poor old guide dog alone to have his snooze.

In the evenings we turn up at functions together and I tell people about the difference my guide dog has made to my life. 'I am now independently mobile,' I explain to those who will listen.

'What do you mean by that?' a perceptive woman asked me once.

'Close your eyes, ma'am,' says I, 'and imagine a world where that is all you can see. Then tell yourself that you deserve to live in a world where you can enjoy the same rights, opportunities and responsibilities as everyone else.' The woman complies. 'Now feel the inadequacy,' I tell her. 'Feel the self-doubt, the cry from within that tells you that this is impossible and that it is unfair and that you need to be cared for.' The woman shifts uncomfortably in her seat. 'Now open your eyes and look at me.'

I have, by now, placed the harness on my dog, I stride forward with the confidence of somebody who has entrusted his safety to a best friend. I hold my hand out. The woman takes it and we shake hands. 'I have crossed the bridge of fear,' I tell her, 'and now I stand on the banks of opportunity. My dog, Martin, sees what I cannot and because he is my friend he will keep me out of harm's way.' The woman pats Martin on the head and he offers her his paw. 'The motivation to accept the possibility of having the same rights, opportunities and responsibilities comes from within. The ability to move around safely is given to be by my guide dog.'

Today I have four wonderful supporters. Mimi is forever a tower of strength and never treats me as a disabled person. 'How about a cup of tea?' I will say in a coaxing way. 'I'd love one,' she will reply and I know instantly that she is not going to allow me to go back behind the shroud that almost destroyed us.

My boys are also doing fine. Stephen, the eldest, is completing his last year studying architecture and he often shows me the drawings he has completed. I place them under special, very powerful, magnifying equipment and I choke with pride at his talent.

'You got it from my Dad,' I tell him. 'He was a great man to draw. He used to draw Roy Rodgers and Billy the Kid and the like.' Then I look at the complexity of expression and feeling in my son's drawings and I realize he is now a professional in his own right.

My youngest son, Adrian, rang me a few months ago. 'Dad,' says he, 'I'm going to be an accountant.' I don't know what it is about us dads but there is something special about having a son that wants to go into the same profession as yourself. I instantly offer him advice. 'Thanks, Da,' says he. 'I'll bear all that in mind.' I know he won't but I felt better for having warned him of all the pitfalls in the profession.

I ring him back. 'Sorry,' says I. 'I met a man called Bob Hayes once and he set me along the road to really under-standing the intricacies of finance. It's a great life and I'll say a prayer you meet your Bob Hayes.'

'Thanks, Da,' says he. 'But you'll do.' I hang up and wipe a tear from my eye. There is something very satisfying about knowing that your children have grown up and are capable of taking the big decisions for themselves.

'God, Martin,' says I, 'but maybe I'm getting old.' He wags his tail and coaxes me towards the front door. 'You're tell-ing me not to get so old that you can't bring me for a run in the woods.' I put on his harness and Mimi, Martin and I cross the road to the woods and Martin runs freely, sniffing the scents of foxes and rabbits as we hold hands and feel lucky at being together.

'We've done okay,' I tell her one day. It was more of a question than a statement of fact.

'We've been very lucky,' she confirms. 'You have a job

where you can make a difference to the lives of people like yourself and you do it well.'

'Do you really mean that?' I ask.

'You have escaped from hell, Tom. Most people never get that opportunity.' I squeeze her hand a little more tightly.

'But you help people as well,' I tell her.

'I do my best,' says she.

'No,' says I. 'You have something that is very rare. You have the ability to give yourself to others without making them feel obligated for the privilege.' This time she squeezes my hand.

In the evenings we sit and watch our favourite television programmes, talk about the books we are reading (in my case listening) and share our love of music. It's a grand life!

I wonder what Aunt Lil would say if she saw me today? I think she would shake my hand and tell me to get down on my knees and thank Himself for giving me the gift of real sight. I now realize that Aunt Lil, who didn't have the professional support offered to me, had cracked the real meaning of that word 'acceptance'.

She was a woman who was at peace with herself and her surroundings. She, like me today, understood the very deep significance of the phrase 'Things are today exactly as they are supposed to be.' There is a great sense of peace in being able to accept this at the deepest level of our souls. But it does require the courage of real humility.

Each Saturday morning I go round to Susanna Menta's house. Susanna is a vibrant Italian violinist who is teaching me classical violin. 'I have never taught a blind person before,' she admitted. 'But I can't see why it should stop you playing music.' With great care and attention to detail Susanna has lifted my playing to a point where I no longer sound like a cat who is seriously ill. Martin no longer runs from the room as I practise except when I play the Ave Maria. This brings back memories of earlier, unbearable squeaking as I tried to master the art of putting my fingers in the right place at the right time.

Ma lives in London now with my brother and loves to hear me play some of the old Irish tunes of our youth. 'Ah, but yer father would be real proud if he could hear ya now,' she would say as I finished playing 'The Old Bog Road' or 'Danny Boy' over the phone to her. We have long chats about the past and she still giggles like a young girl at the things we got up to as kids. 'Lord, but ya were divils,' she says.

I still want to do more and my employers, the Guide Dogs for the Blind Association, realize the enormity of the task. Over the next five years it is seeking to expand its services to visually impaired people but will still remain the world's largest and best provider of guide dogs like Martin. 'I'm in me element,' as John-Joe would have said.

Every day I meet other guide dog owners like myself, and the power of identification that comes from sharing our stories, hopes and strengths is very healing. I wake up in the mornings wanting to go to work, wanting to do more but understanding that the journey through blindness is one that we must all take alone. All that people like Brian Cooney and I can do is feel privileged that for a few moments along the way a person who is coping with their journey from the dark will stop and chat, and maybe hear something that will remove their particular veil that traps them inside of themselves.

My home town of Birr is as beautiful as ever. The purple-hued mountains now vibrate for me with the music of the Marian Ceili Band and the roars of the crowds as they demanded an encore from Dad and me. Our home has become a supermarket but I still meet some of the people who used to come to our shop. They, like me, are a little older but a lot wiser.

Martin stirs in his bed beneath my desk in the study. 'Aren't you finished yet?' he moans.

'I just have a few more lines to write,' I tell him, 'then I'll turn off the light.' He scratches his ear in disbelief.

It's around ten o'clock and the house is still except for the sound of the central heating. At times like this, when I am alone with myself, I agree with what Aunt Lil told me. Blindness is one of the worst disabilities that can be visited on a human being. So many of life's pleasures are visual and no matter how I try to say that I accept my blindness and its consequences, I still miss being able to see the actors on a stage, to watch their expressions, or their detailed hand movements. Sometimes I even resent having to construct what I think they might be from visual memory. It is as if life has become one long radio play.

I curse myself when I am unable to distinguish brown

socks from black or a yellow shirt from a white one, or when one of my children cuts their finger and asks me to look at it. I scream inside when I would like to roam freely in a bookshop and to select a book of my choice, bring it home and savour the smell of a good read. My loss of sight has robbed me of this simple pleasure.

I miss New York and Boston and that feeling of latent excitement that invites you to be a part of it. My strolls on Wall Street still seem filled with a clarion cry to join the forces of the laterally thinking. But I can see their focus no more.

Yet, if I were to go back to that time when Julie urged me to tell Peter the truth about my sight loss, would I now do it? Yes. I would. But not so that I could turn the clock back and once again become part of the dark-suited world of finance. I would tell him the truth because that is the right thing to do with a friend and Peter was, is and always will be a good friend to me.

Martin shifts position in his bed. He is reminding me that he is still there and that it is time to put out the light. 'Just a few minutes more,' I tell him.

I do not want to turn back the clock on any aspect of my life. To do so would be to deny this Saul on the road to Damascus type journey that is my life. The journey may not be as I would like it to be in all of its details and there are some aspects of it that I would have liked Him to have planned a little better, but it's a really good life.

Today, my love of writing is all consuming and I hanker for times, like now, when the house is quiet and my spirit is still. I lift my pen and write from memory about places I have visited and people I have met. I am visited by characters who demand space on my pages and they tell me about their adventures. Perhaps, one day, I can tell you their stories.

Bang! You're Dead

Technology is advancing and it is only a matter of time until science finds a replacement for lost vision. I want to be a part of this quest. Not for the selfish reason of replacing my own lost sight but because I believe it can be done and that somewhere out there is a person who can do it. What a fantastic expedition it will be to find him or her. It will be like Stanley meeting Livingstone in the jungle. I would be so proud to have the honour of repeating those well-worn words.

The unemployment rate amongst blind people continues to soar and there is much work to be done to convince employers that it is alright to hire a blind person. We may look a little odd but we're as keen as mustard.

Thousands of people who become blind each day need people like me to help them through their journey towards acceptance. Once they have crossed over the bridge of anger and want to continue to live a life that is filled with as much normality as possible, they will need a guide dog just like Martin. I want to be there when that happens.

I scratch Martin behind the ear and wish him goodnight. I turn out the light and make my way to bed. 'Thank you, God,' I pray, 'for the serenity I have felt today.' I close my eyes and think of Birr.

'Bang! You're dead,' says Jimmy.
'Feck off,' says I, 'I'm too busy to die.'

Guide Dogs

John Wiley and Sons Ltd, the publishers of Bang! You're Dead are delighted to support the Guide Dogs for the Blind Association by donating 5% of revenue received by them from the sale of this book to the Association.

The Guide Dogs for the Blind Association

The Guide Dogs for the Blind Association provides guide dogs, mobility and other rehabilitation services that meet the needs of blind and partially sighted people. They also provide free long cane and low vision training to visually impaired people.

Guide Dogs is the world's largest breeder and trainer of working dogs and every year around 1200 would-be guide dogs are born at home to our brood bitches, specially chosen for their intelligence and temperament. The lifetime cost of each guide dog is £35,000 including all its vet and food bills.

For the last five years, the Guide Dogs has been the UK's largest single provider of funds for research into dog health issues. It is also contributing five million pounds towards human ophthalmic research over the next seven years.

The Guide Dogs rely entirely on public generosity to fund their vital work.